Why Wicca

Rowan Antinous

Published by Exultans Publishers, 2025.

While every precaution has been taken in the preparation of this book, the publisher assumes no responsibility for errors or omissions, or for damages resulting from the use of the information contained herein.

WHY WICCA

First edition. May 24, 2025.

Copyright © 2025 Rowan Antinous.

ISBN: 979-8988483458

Written by Rowan Antinous.

Table of Contents

Why Wicca 1

Dedication 2

Foreword 4

Section One - History of the Faith (Goddess Worship) | Chapter One: The Paleolithic 11

Chapter Two - The Mesolithic and Neolithic 22

Chapter Three – Bronze Age and pre-Modern 31

Chapter Four – Endurance 38

Section Two – The Modern Day | Chapter Five – Reemergence 42

Chapter Six - Wicca Today 46

Section 3 – Ritual Practice: solitary and group | Chapter Seven – Statements of Faith 57

Chapter Eight – Holy Days, the Great Wheel 66

Chapter Nine – Rituals and Ritual Practice 71

Chapter Ten - New Aeon Generic Ritual Outline – 97

Chapter Eleven – Sample Rituals from Various Traditions 105

Chapter Twelve - Various Special Rituals. 145

Chapter Thirteen – Occasional Rituals 173

Chapter Fourteen – Wiccan Apologetics 210

Appendix B – 252

Appendix C – 255

Appendix D – 265

Appendix E – 268

Appendix F – 274

Appendix G – 276

Appendix H – 281

Appendix I – 283

Part One – | Chapter One: 297

Chapter Two: 298

Chapter Three: 299

Chapter Four: 301

Chapter Five: 302

Chapter Six: 303

Part Two – | Chapter Eight: 304

Why Wicca?

The Developed World's Fastest Growing Religion

By the Reverend Rowan Antinous

Under guidance from

The Extremely Reverend Davron Michaels (Paramount priest- Church of the New Aeon)

The Extremely Reverend Ruthann Amartefio (late Archpriestess - Church of the New Aeon)

Copyright © 2025 Exultans Publishing.

Published by Exultans Publishing

All rights reserved. This book or any portion thereof may not be reproduced or used in any manner whatsoever without the express written permission of the publisher.

Approved for use by The New Aeon Church, International

(The New Aeon Church, International is an Omnistic Faith Tradition which embraces all positive faith. This is the first of a series of "Why" Books regarding different faiths and why people might choose them.)

Dedication

This book is dedicated to all seekers, but particularly to the Extremely Reverend Ruthann Amarteifo, who has passed the veil and departed from this plane. May she rest in the Light and return to the Wheel renewed, or pass on into the Summerlands to dwell forever.

Foreword

We certainly hope that you enjoy reading this book and studying about Wicca. I have approached this work as a combination of scholarship and liturgy.

By this I mean that the first section of the book, consisting of a number of chapters, studies the history of goddess worship through the ages, ending with the emergence of Wicca as a modern faith. These chapters are treated as a scholarly work and contain citations, and reference lists. I have attempted to make them readable and believe that I have succeeded, however, they are also intended to be a genuine history of what we know about goddess worship, from the stone age to the present day, and I have written them to be defensible as such.

The later sections cover, in the second section, the practices of the faith itself as it is followed by both solitary practitioners and "congregations," and the third section covers the challenges that face the faith going forward and topics like apologetics (defense of the faith). That third section was hard to write comprehensively, but we sincerely hope that you find it useful..

Why do I not say covens? Because honestly, Wicca is not just or even mostly covens. There are covens in it - but there are also significant groups that don't claim any lineages and that function exactly like congregations in any faith. Let us also be clear, Wicca is a form of neoPaganism. So while all Wiccans are at some level neoPagans, not all neoPagans are Wiccan. "Witches" are also often conflated with Wiccans, but, while some "witches" are Wiccans, not all Wiccans are "witches." In fact, from what I have seen, a minority of Wiccans are witches, and some neoPagans and some "witches" take umbrage at being called Wiccan, in fact.

I am an Omnist (I respect all good faiths - many paths, one goal) and I have attended four different neoPagan groups over the last twenty (20) years, while also attending other faith communities as well, particularly Episcopalian and on occasion Catholic. Reverend Doctor Timothy Lake's group was called a "cluster," and I've seen so many people in the meeting space for that cluster that it was impossible to move.. That group was distinctly Wiccan, although Tim himself is Asatru. If it had been advertised as something other than Wiccan, I probably would never have attended. Over a hundred and fifty people called it their spiritual home. Tim very much functioned as a clergyman as well as leading the rituals. He was where people went, even if they didn't attend the services, when they needed help. He even opened city council meetings in Schenectady, NY once or twice, as a member of the interfaith group in the city.

The second and third groups we attended were also congregations, without any question. The second met in an old Spiritualist church that they were trying to buy. Average services ranged between 30 and 60 people, occasionally more. It was active in the local interfaith movement, and again, there was a leader who functioned as clergy as well as ritualist. The third group was the remnant of the second group after the purchase attempt was scuttled and we lost the building to meet in. We met at a rented space and the group was consistently 20 to 40 attendees.

Finally, after we moved to the country, the fourth group, which I still sometimes attend, is smaller, perhaps a dozen people. It is differentiated by its priestess as neoPagan, specifically. The rituals however are largely in line with what I have seen consistently in Wicca. We live in a rural area and community building is not something that has been aggressively pursued. I attempted to find a local interfaith movement and largely discovered that there were not even interfaith services between Christian churches - and that many of them don't even have answering machines, say nothing about a public face. Nevertheless, we have certification as a recognized faith group and we go on our way.

For many people, this is not what they imagine Wicca or neoPaganism to be like. The reality is however, that in not a single one of the groups were more than a tiny handful of the attendees practitioners of "witchcraft" or any of the other things that are commonly associated with Wiccans and neoPagans. Most were pew sitters, exactly like the pew sitters in any congregation of any faith. I am usually a pew sitter wherever I am, although I am ordained via multiple paths - Christian, Universalist and Metaphysical. I know lots of theory and a whole lot of theology (thus my writing this book) - but - it's a faith, nothing more or less to me. Whether it was Tim (Dr. Lake) or Father Stan (may he rest in Light) or whoever, the person who leads the ritual is usually a capable practitioner, but most of us are there for the service as part of a community of faith, or as in most churches, not even of that particular faith but coming with family.

This should not be a surprise to anyone. Afterall, those who followed the various precursors to Wicca were not ceremonialists. They were the villagers, the farmers, the hunters, the people, and those that they looked to, who led the solstices and the services were, very much like the clergy in other faiths are today, the only ones who necessarily knew why or how the rituals worked, who were, often, casting spells exactly like a good priest leads prayer for the people. The fact that they were ceremonial magicians, well, even if the words are never used, so are most clergy today, by action and intention if not by title.

The antecedents of Wicca were not elites, they were common workers, warriors, farmers and goodwives. This book honors Wicca and its antecedents as a faith. There are certainly mystery schools within it, and without it, just as there are within and without more modern, monotheistic faiths - but it is a religion, just as its ancestor faiths were.

Blessed be.

i

Prologue (*by the Paramount Priest of the Church of the New Aeon, International*)

In recent decades, the landscape of religious affiliation has undergone a profound transformation. Traditional religious institutions, once the bedrock of communal and spiritual life, have witnessed a marked decline in participation. This shift is driven by a confluence of factors: secularization, the rise of individualism, cultural evolution, disillusionment with religious institutions, economic stability, technological advancements, generational changes, and political polarization. Moreover, issues like gender-based exclusion and the rigid dogmas of organized religions have led many to seek spiritual fulfillment outside conventional frameworks. These societal shifts reflect a broader change in how individuals view religion, spirituality, and the role these play in their lives.

In response to this changing spiritual landscape, new forms of religious expression and community have emerged. Among them is the New Aeon Church, a modern Omnistic community that offers an inclusive and adaptable approach to spirituality and worship. The New Aeon Church stands as a beacon for those who wish to explore and integrate diverse spiritual traditions, creating a space where thousands of members—each with their own unique beliefs and practices—come together under a common umbrella to worship, share, and grow.

At the heart of the New Aeon Church is the concept of Omnism. Omnism is a worldview that embraces the idea that truth and wisdom are not confined to a single religious tradition but can be found across all religions and spiritual practices. It is a philosophy marked by respect for diverse beliefs, an inclusive approach to spirituality, and a non-dogmatic stance that encourages personal exploration. Omnists seek to understand and appreciate the commonalities and unique insights of various religious practices, fostering a sense of unity and mutual respect among people of different faiths.

Unlike traditional religious institutions, the New Aeon Church recognizes the importance of individual spiritual autonomy. Members are encouraged to define and construct their own belief systems, with guidance from dedicated clergy who help shape and refine these personal paths within an overarching Omnistic framework. Some congregants have crafted entirely unique and personal systems of belief and practice, while others find fulfillment within one of the more structured, yet still flexible, Orders, such as the Order of Wicca.

The New Aeon Wiccan Tradition is one of the largest and fastest-growing components within the Church. Wicca, a modern pagan religion, venerates nature, celebrates the cyclical rhythms of the seasons, and incorporates ritual magic and polytheistic worship. It is a path that encourages harm-free living, personal responsibility, and ethical awareness. Wicca's practices are often highly personalized, allowing adherents to tailor their rituals and beliefs to align with their individual spiritual needs.

Wicca's appeal to modern spiritual seekers is multifaceted. Its deep connection to nature resonates with those yearning for a more harmonious relationship with the Earth. Its flexibility and emphasis on personal empowerment provide a sense of agency in one's spiritual journey. The religion's feminist and inclusive values offer an alternative to the patriarchal structures of many traditional religions, making it particularly attractive to those seeking equality and representation. Moreover, Wicca's rich ritual practices and accessibility offer a tangible, meaningful way to engage with both the world and the divine.

In a world where many are searching for spiritual paths that resonate with contemporary values and personal experiences, Omnistic Wicca offers a compelling alternative. It is a tradition that honors diversity, encourages exploration, and fosters a deep, meaningful connection with the natural and spiritual world. As you embark on the journey through this book, you will discover the principles, practices, and profound wisdom that Omnistic Wicca brings to the modern spiritual seeker.

–The Most Reverend Davron Michaels

Table of Contents

Section One - History of the Faith (Goddess Worship)

Chapter One: The Paleolithic

The Prehistory of mankind begins about 2.5 million years ago and continues until about 1200 BCE. That entire period is subdivided into three "ages" by experts. The Stone Age, the Bronze Age and the Iron Age. The Stone Age, which takes up most of that time, is itself subdivided into three parts as well. The Paleolithic (early Stone Age), the Mesolithic (middle Stone Age) and Neolithic (New Stone Age). The Paleolithic part ends in 10,000 BCE

The earliest piece of identifiable and fully recognized religious art is from the Upper Paleolithic period. The Venus of Willendorf was discovered on "the left bank of the Danube in Willendorf II/Lower Austria on August 7th, 1908 during excavations led by Josef Szombathy, supervised by Hugo Obermaier and Josef Bayer" (Weber, et al., 2022, Para. 2). [see fig 2-1] The Venus of Willendorf is dated to between 24,000 and 22,000 BCE. It is not the oldest Venus figurine, but was the first one universally recognized by experts as being a religious figurine.

Figure 2-1

The Venus of Hohle Fels dates to between 38,000 and 33,000 BCE. [see fig 2-2 in "Illustrations"] While the Venus of Hohle Fels is also almost certainly a goddess figurine, that was not as widely accepted as the character of the Venus of Willendorf is by scholars at the time of discovery. Instead, because some scholars did not believe that religion existed until about that time, they viewed the Venus of Hohle Fels as a simple representation of a human female. This was asserted, even by some scholars that believe the same culture created religion that created the Venus of Hohle Fels.

The Venus of Hohle Fels (also known as the Venus of Schelklingen) was found more recently than the Venus of Willendorf, being uncovered in the area of Schelklingen, Germany in 2008. The Venus of Hohle Fels is carved from mammoth tusk and is part of a cache of figures found in the caves in the area at the time.

Figure 2-2While, as we have noted, there are those who asserted that it was simply art, there were others, a majority, like the anthropologists from the University of Wellington, who asserted almost at once that the figure "represented "hope for survival and longevity, within well-nourished and reproductively successful communities." Thus matching historic expectations for fertility and mother goddess figures. "Certainly" most scholars agreed, the interpretation of the Venus of Hohle Fels is generally that of a fertility or mother goddess. This is supported by the large bust and ample proportions of the figure, which "resemble later, well proven, goddess figures."

So with the Venus of Hohle Fels our knowledge of goddess figures goes back further into the past than it does due to the Venus of Willendorf, by a minimum of 9,000 years.

Of course there are other Venus figurines as well. Between the Venus of Hohle Fels and the Venus of Willendorf are many others. The Venus of Dolni Vestonice for example. She was carved about 30,000 years ago in the Moravian basin (Czech Republic). There are literally hundreds, possibly thousands of Venus figurines, carved in rock, ivory, and almost every other material imaginable that have been found (a small selection of Venus figurines side by side can be seen in fig 2-3). It is reasonable to assume that there are thousands more not yet discovered.

Figure 2-3

Compellingly, there are "Venus figurines" even older than any of these, even older than Hohle Fels.

The oldest known Venus figurines are a pair, the Venus of Berekhat Ram was found lodged between two geologic strata of volcanic residue[1], the upper one dating to 230,000 BCE and the lower one dating to 700,000 BCE. This neatly proves that the figurine was created somewhere between those two dates, though we cannot be sure at which end of the gap.

Initially, archeologists were not certain, or to be more realistic did not want the Venus of Berekhat Ram to be an actual Venus. The preference of researchers was that it was a naturally eroded rock. Two things have settled the question however.

The first is a second figurine. A second figurine, showing the same features and design, was found on the north bank of the River Draa a few kilometers south of the Moroccan town of Tan-Tan. The Venus of Tan-Tan, dated according to the strata in which it was found, was created between 300,000 BCE and 500,000 BCE. Since that appears contemporaneous with the Venus of Berekhat Ram, this probably indicates that the Venus of Berekhat Ram was also created in that part of the larger range given by its sandwiching in the strata.

The second compelling discovery that settled questions about the Venus of Berekhat Ram, and now its cousin, the Venus of Tan-Tan, is that specialized microscopic examination showed artificial tool marks, apparently made by very sharp slivers of stone, used to mark the limbs and other parts of the figurines, in particular the Berekhat Ram (d'Errico, F., 2000).

[a picture of the Venus of Berekhat Ram can be seen in Fig 2-4; a picture of the Venus of Tan-Tan can be seen in Fig 2-5]

These two Venus figurines, rough, primitive, basic were not, in fact could not have been created by modern man or Neandrathal. They were created by Homo Erectus, it is generally believed. The same archeologists who will claim any unknown or mysterious structure, space, or statue must have been ceremonial or religious are only slowly coming to recognize that these Venus figurines, as early and primitive as they are, were certainly devotional objects. Votive statues, if you would, long before the Greco Roman period that we for so long thought gave birth to the concept.

Figure 2-4

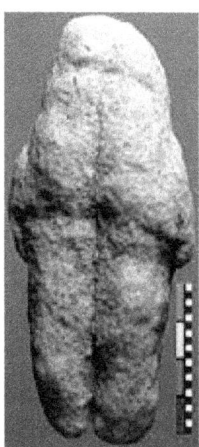
Figure 2-5

The evidence is overwhelming. Humans, throughout our history and the history of our precursor species, worshiped the divine feminine. They made figurines intended to invite the blessing of goddesses on their clans and tribes, particularly the blessings of fertility and safe birth. Worship of a mother goddess is not a new idea. It is, ironically, older than homo sapien sapien, or if you prefer, older than modern man.

What is NOT extremely evident until very recently, are gods. Male figures that had the same importance to the people of the time that the goddess figures did. One could argue that worshiping the hunting spirits was important, because hunters provided protein for the tribe or clan. That seems as if it should be extremely important, given that more than 65% of early human groups gained more than 50% of their calories, as well as their protein, from animal products (Cordain, *et al.*, 2000). One could also argue that worshiping male fertility deities was also as important as worshiping female ones - however, the evidence found to date does not support either of those assertions.

There is only one significant male statue of similar age to Hohle Fels, and that is The Lion-man of Hohlenstein-Stadel. Also carved from Mammoth Ivory, the Lion-man is zoomorphic (figure 2-6) and was carved approximately 35,000 years ago. It is possible that it represented a god, but if so, a hunting god, and a very different type of deity than the mother goddess/fertility goddess that we see in the Venus statues.

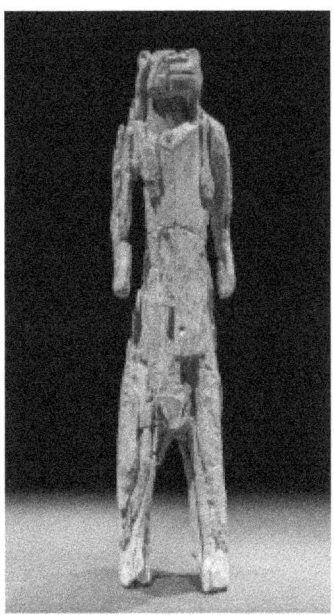
Figure 2-6

It is noteworthy that there was also an ivory phallus found, from the same period, called the phallus of Hohle Fels, and found in the same caves that gave up the Venus of Hohle Fels. A male symbol of fertility that, as we know, has endured through the ages, but rather than showing the spiritual longing, the reaching for the comfort of a supernal mother goddess, the phallus instead shows the self-centered, self-worship/penis worship of men. Mind you, I have no objection to penis worship, but I do agree that when a man cries out "O my God" when orgasming he is actually calling his penis his god - and I think that is alright. It is not, however, the same as praying to a divine source for comfort, peace, successful birth, and calling for the life of your offspring and the survival of your people. (there will be no illustration of the Phallus of Hohle Fels - because of the possibility of offending the parents of any minors reading this)

This is not to suggest that the divine masculine is not equally important, it is to say that its worship was established much later than the worship of the divine feminine.

Chapter Two - The Mesolithic and Neolithic

This second section of the Stone Age, the Mesolithic, stretches from 10,000 BCE to 8,000 BCE - a much shorter run than its hoary older sibling. The Neolithic stretches from 8,000 (10,000 in some chronologies) BCE to about 2,000 BCE (3,500 in some chronologies). Then the timeline gives way to the Copper Age (Chalcolithic Age), although to further confuse things, some experts consider there to be an overlap between neolithic and chalcolithic running from about 3500 to about 2300 BCE, where either name can be legitimately used.

Figure 3-1 During this period of time, evidence for empowered goddess worship continues to strongly present itself. Nowhere more strongly than in the archeological dig at Catal Hoyük. Goddess worship was prominent in the city of Catal Hoyük. There was a shrine in the city for every four or five houses and nearly all of those shrines were dedicated to a, or possibly then, the goddess. Goddess figures, both painted and sculpted, were found throughout the dig. At first archeologists assumed that they were incidental or toys or... and then the number of images, and number of shrines celebrating pregnant, or birthing females

simply overwhelmed them, and many gave way to reality. At this point it is almost universally accepted that Catal Hoyük was a center for goddess worship, and that is reinforced by the more than 700 goddess statues that have been found there.

Figure 3-1 shows an obese woman,[2] seated on a primitive throne, with animals, most likely leopards,[3] on either side of her. This is not an uncommon type of statue in this period. In fact, dozens of this female figure, often in the midst of giving birth, have been found in the dig. Some made of clay, some of limestone, etc. Often they are accompanied by or even riding, leopards.

Others have been found, like Figure 3-2, which are obviously the same woman, but standing.

Figure 3-2

Now of course, there are arguments against any of these being goddesses, some from traditional archeologists, but of course, most tellingly from members of patriarchal religions. Let's take a brief look at some of the objections.

Tinning (2017) notes that "experts on prehistoric art warn that we shouldn't read too much into these figurines, and suggest that they may simply have been creating art for art's sake." Later in the article Tinning forwards the question of whether or not the inclusion of the finding of male and animal figurines at the time of the announcement of the finding of female figurines would have changed the media response.

Doing a bit of research, I was able to find images of a bearded man in a swing (Figure 3-3) and quite a few animals, including what appears to be the equivalent of a farm play set, but very very few verified males, other than animals, which hardly are the same, but as noted prior, related to the hunting of meat, which continued to provide a large portion of the calories and nearly all of the protein.

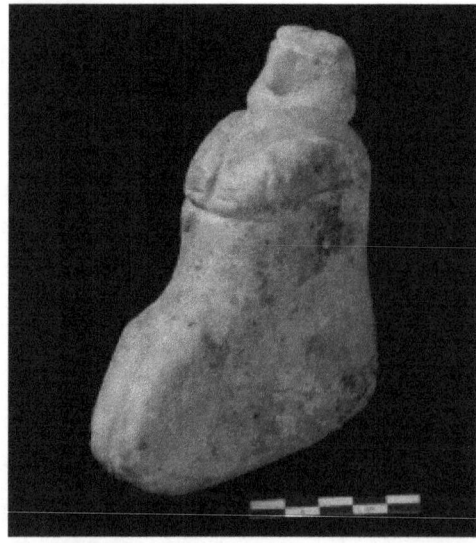

Figure 3-3

Figure 3-4

Let me note, that there were some additional male figures including one found in shrine E VI (Figure 3-4) which appears to be a young man or boy from comparative sizing and what can be made out of the body shape.

WHY WICCA

Figure 3-5

Most things found representing men however, are like Figure 3-5, related to, as I have previously mentioned, hunting.

Why, you wonder, is such an effort made to discredit the finding of female votive statues at Cataloyuk? I believe that the reasons are threefold.

1. The traditional male domination of modern culture, while fraying, remains, and it bothers many archeologists to find evidence that it was not always so.
2. Archeology, like all of the sciences, changes very slowly. How slowly? There is an old saying in many STEM fields that change comes one death at a time. It sounds morbid, but it is somewhat accurate. Older academics and scientists, who have made their reputations and legacies with a particular theory in a particular field are loath to see that theory challenged, because it affects them.
3. Religion. Modern religion, particularly Abrahamic religion, is fiercely patriarchal. Abrahamic religion is certainly no more than 5,000 years old, and I think much younger than that[4]. Having it accepted that there was goddess worship or even egalitarian worship, tens of thousands of years earlier than that is a poke in the eye. People poked in the eye tend to poke back. Thus articles like "Catalhoyuk home to figurines of old women, not goddesses" in the *Daily Sabah* - a Right wing pro government Turkish paper are, though they would never say it, those poke-backs.

Unfortunately for those with injured posteriors, there is significant other evidence of goddess worship in the neolithic period. In fact, since there are records from the end of the neolithic period in India and remains from the Indus Valley civilization as well that we can examine, it seems that goddess worship can be established despite the objections.

In the Indus Valley Civilization (3300 - 1300 BCE; mature 2600-1900 BCE), there were over 1000 cities and settlements that have been identified. There are seals with images of people (possibly gods) and undeciphered script from the Indus Valley writing system. The existence of evidence, particularly in the remains of the city of Harappa, suggests that the people worshiped a goddess, probably a mother goddess. This pre Hindu faith, also included what appear to be proto-Phallic symbology.[5] In fact, this may well have been the cradle of modern Hinduism. Within it, the presence of a strong female goddess is extremely compelling, and difficult to discard.

Not that there are no attempts of course. Ratnagar (2016) argues that the statues in Mohenjo Daro (another Indus Valley city) are not really goddesses, but are just women doing household chores, or having babies, or whatever - no matter what numbers they have. He argues that they are most likely shamanistic figures, used in rituals to ward off evil spirits and not truly "divine." Homemade representations of women to ward off those evil forces, and not idols of the Mother Goddess, or of a goddess at all.

So to step back and take a look at the whole. We have very similar representations of a female fertility figure from at least 35,000 BCE until at least the end of the neolithic period in 2,000 BCE. Clear female representations broadly believed to be votive statues, but not accepted as such by a small body of regressive scholars and religious leaders. In those same periods of time, male representations either relate to hunting or with very few exceptions are purely sexual, in the sense that, a phallus is not a male person, we may, as I have noted, worship our penises during intercourse of whatever type and orgasm, but they are not people.

The argument that all of the female representations found, most of which resemble corpulent women, in a way clearly identifiable as indicating success and reproduction, are something else in their hundreds, or thousands, other than goddesses; when the exact same archeologists attempt to make nearly everything else they find out to be a ritual item or a cult device, strains credulity.

To put it simply, bull. We know that shamanism existed, and we know that it overlaps other forms of worship, just fine. We know that the traditional evolution of religion, as seen by most scholars, is animism to spiritism to deism, to polytheism, to monotheism, possibly with henotheism thrown in between poly- and mono-theism. In that schema the first group that seem to have moved from spiritism to deism is goddesses. That is a fact.

Chapter Three – Bronze Age and pre-Modern

As we emerge into the Bronze Age we see religion beginning to take a new form. Many scholars think that agriculture is the cause for this. As agriculture gets more and more complicated, it is harder for pregnant women to engage in it, and so they begin to lose status. The loss is gradual however, and slow. Many ancient cultures simply reimagined women's place, often connecting them to earth and water as the symbology of the elements began to develop (Behjati-Ardakani, *et al*, 2016). But quite often, the priesthoods of the gods were not content. The emergence of nation-states, often male dominated, also hastened the change (Rohrlich, 1980)

Of course, the changes in culture and in the interaction of the people with the earth was reflected in other ways as well. The struggle between hunting, or herding, and cultivation is particularly evident in the myth of Cain and Abel. Yet, the most recent incarnations of that ancient struggle were in the 1800s in the Southwest of the United States. So it was not just changes in the status or power of women that emerged out of the change from a hunter-gatherer society to an agricultural one, and from nomadic existence to urban.

Goddesses began to decline. They became the consorts and daughters of major gods in many cases, although some of them retained their independence and power. Inanna from the Sumerian myth, Likewise Nin.har.sag. No one could keep Inanna and her priestesses under control. That is of course the basis of a centuries long struggle against Inanna, and those other goddesses, like Astarte, and Ishtar, and possibly even Lilith, who were actually or may have been Inanna under other names. It is the basis for many myths that remain in different forms to this day. It also led to marvelous poems, often considered the earliest religious songs or psalms. "*The Courtship of Inanna and Dumuzi*" and "*The Descent of Ishtar*" are examples. *The Courtship* is a rollicking and very sexual tale of the goddess, often acted out by her high priestess with the king, wherein *The Descent* is a song in which the goddess descends into the underworld, which is ruled by her sister, and is temporarily trapped there. (Appendix One contains the full text of the sacred songs.)

Figure 4-1 Goddess Inanna

Nevertheless, goddesses endured as nearly all nations became polytheistic, or in some cases henotheistic.[6] Inanna's cult spread far from its cult center at Uruk and was celebrated in many other cities as well, including Nippur, Isin, Kisurra and Babylon, with region specific versions such as Inanna of Zabalam. As has previously been mentioned, incarnations of the Queen of Heaven, which was her official title, spread with other names as well, Ishtar, Astarte, possibly Lilith (first wife of Adam in some Talmudic traditions) and even, according to some scholars, Isis. They see the overlapping stories of Inanna's descent into the underworld and Isis' resurrection or partial resurrection of Osiris to be strong evidence that the goddess Isis is another avatar of Inanna or at least repeats her stories. (Kujawa, nd) After all, the story of Inanna is at least 4300 years old, and may be older, while the story of Isis can be traced to about that same time frame with more certainty. (Hausman & Boggs, 2022)

Of course, when we look outside the West, we find goddesses a plenty in other period religions. In China, where Wangmu Niangniang, the Queen Mother of the West, is commonly viewed as the most powerful goddess, with complete control over life, happiness, and immortality. Likewise, Guan Yin, Goddess of Mercy is still beloved, having eleven heads to hear all of the cries of the people, and 1000 arms to comfort them. She is viewed as limitless and unstoppable, and is believed to be able to appear in any form at any time. Goddess Nuwa also remains popular to this day. The creator of mankind, she is believed to be the first being with the ability to procreate and is thought to be the originator of all human life on earth. As a fertility goddess, she more closely resembles the fertility goddesses of other parts of the world at the time of her origin, like Inanna.

Hinduism, with its aforementioned close apparent ties to the Indus Valley civilization also has quite a number of goddesses that reach back into the Bronze age. Furthermore, in the Hindu faith, goddesses alone can be the mother of the universe, and they alone possess the power of creating and destroying the world. Many Hindus believe that all the goddesses are different aspects of the supreme goddess Adi Shakti. Regardless they are worshiped separately and include such beings as Bhuvaneshwari, the prime force of the world. Annapurna, who can provide food to an infinite number of people and of course goddess Durga, the ultimate mother goddess.

Unlike most religions however, Hinduism appears to have developed out of the ancient goddess and the phallus that we mentioned in earlier days, to become fairly egalitarian but deeply wound up in the intertwining of the gods and goddesses, or perhaps more accurately of the masculine and feminine energies. To this day the goddesses are viewed as being the creators, and the divine "shakti" of the gods, in the form of their wives, together with the fact that the great deities of Hinduism are often androgynous, because Hinduism views the divine as neither male nor female, but both. It also views the divine as not formless or embodied, but both. This outlook reemerges in many forms of modern neoPaganism, New Age mysticism, and Wicca.

When we look at native and First People's cultures and native religions around the world it is often difficult to determine how old a particular goddess is. The indigenous religions were orally transmitted, and sometimes were part of secret society rituals within the tribes. That makes determining how old a particular deity is, in terms of its worship, very tricky. It is safe to say however that all of the traditional goddesses had been worshiped for some time before invaders came, and so it is reasonable to assume that most of them were entrenched as faiths for their tribes and people during the late bronze age at least, and certainly in the iron age.

Among the various indigenous American tribes, there were many goddesses, often supreme. Among the Cherokee, for example, Unelanuhi, the sun goddess presided over all things, made the earth and provided for her people, Unelanuhi was and is believed to be all-seeing, all-knowing, and all-powerful. Interestingly, the very traits that modern monotheists apply to their deities. (Hunt, 2001 ; Mooney, 1966). Among the Algonquin, Nokomis was goddess of the earth, or earth mother. That role is filled by Cihuacoatl among the Aztec, and by Nujalik, who is also goddess of the hunt among the Inuit of Alaska and by Ataensic among the Huron, a worship shared by the Iroquois confederacy and its tribes. The Hopi saluted Ragno - a mother goddess, a position held in the Navajo pantheon by Iyatiku, who holds the same position among the Pueblo. The Navajo also have a supreme or chief goddess, named Estananethehi; they do not share her with the Pueblo.

Figure 4-2 (Burial inscription from Khirbet el-Quom, 8th century BCE. Museum of Israel: "Blessed be Uriyahu by Yahweh and his Asherah, for from his enemies he has saved him.")

Many books could be filled with the names and what we know of the stories of goddesses. Despite the loss of power over time, goddesses continued to be worshiped, in Judaism, as it moved from Henotheism to genuine monotheism, a goddess survived in the form of Sophia (the Greek name for Wisdom) and another in the form of "God's wife" Asherah. (Viegas, 2011) [7]

Figure 4-2

As strange as this may sound to modern ears. Many scholars believe that El, a Canaanite god, was originally the ruling god of a pantheon of his children, with Asherah, his wife. In the Bible, El "El Elyon" (god most high) is referred to as the leader of the divine council, and it is said that he grants the people of Israel to YHWH (Yahweh) as his "portion." (Deuteronomy 32:8-9). The nearest we have to the original translates those verses roughly as: "When *Elyon* apportioned the nations, when he divided the *b'nei Adam*, he fixed the boundaries of the peoples according to the number of the *b'nei Elohim;* YHVH's own portion was his people, Jacob his allotted share." Another Hebrew translation says "When Elyon gave the nations as an inheritance, when he separated the sons of man, he set the boundaries of the peoples according to the number of **the sons of God** (bny 'l[hym]). For Yahweh's portion was his people; Jacob was the lot of his inheritance".'"

Yahweh was apparently one of El Elyon's children, originally probably a mountain god, he was, in the divine council, given power over the people of Israel by El (something easily established in the received texts today and further supported by the Dead Sea Scrolls - which clearly demonstrate that they were viewed as separate gods - no matter what modern apologists would have us believe)(Heiser, 2006). The reconstruction suggests that over time, Yahweh, due to Israel (Jacob, his portion), equalled El, surpassed him, and became chief god, at which time he inherited Asherah as his wife.

Even by the time the priesthood collated the stories into scripture, Asherah had not been fully suppressed. Thus you get verses like Deuteronomy 33:2-3, which reads in the oldest versions we have: *"YHWH came from Sinai,and shone forth from his own Seir, He showed himself from Mount Paran. Yea, he came among the myriads of Qudhsu, at his right hand his own Asherah, Indeed, he who loves the clans and all his holy ones on his left."* (Dukstra M, 2001) Now, this is obviously not what most modern Bibles read, and that is for the simple reason that over and over editors have changed the scriptures to better match what they want them to say, it is frustrating in the extreme, but it is reality. You can also see the battle for control of the Jewish people in 2nd Kings of course.

Put aside the idea that any of it was divine or anything other than power play and read Chapter 23, verse 7. "He also tore down the quarters of the male shrine prostitutes that were in the temple of the LORD, the quarters where women did weaving for Asherah." So in that single verse we see that women wove garments for Asherah AND that there were male shrine prostitutes at the Temple, and had been for a long time, probably from the beginning of the faith.

Anyway, as late as the late Iron Age, the worship of goddesses was alive and well.

Then, in the West, came Christianity. Christianity made a few changes in general. They attempted to make the final leap out of henotheism, but in order to compete with the Zoroastrians, they needed dualism, so they created a weak dualism by elevating Satan, who in Judaism was viewed as a lawyer assigned by G-d to advocate against G-d, and made him into the figure we see today. To handle the goddess challenge they elevated Mary, the Mother of Christ and gave her titles originally belonging to Inanna, who was, you may remember, the Queen of Heaven," but they also made her "evervirgin" which as you can see from the sacred poems, Inanna was anything but.

The goddesses were finally, in the minds of the priesthood, put in their place, a placing that continued in later Abrahamic faiths. Islam continued to recognize Mary, even as they reduced her son to the status of a prophet, and only in Mormonism do you find something of a return to goddesses. Despite their strictly patriarchal nature, they acknowledge divine sex and the existence of "God's wife" (or wives), who is (are) the mother(s) of the spirits of human beings (Noyce, 2016; Fletcher-Stack, 2021).

Nevertheless, during the "age of the church," Church fathers sought to crush out all pagan faiths, including goddess worship, other than the salutation of Mary, who they claimed was not a goddess. Sophia was reduced to the spirit of wisdom, and Asherah was eternally relegated to being a pole. With the other large Abrahamic faith also engaged in the destruction of the pagan faiths and certainly all worship of goddesses, it seemed as if the divine feminine, along with polytheism were being relegated to the dustbin of history.

Chapter Four – Endurance

Firstly, a mother goddess and her son was not a new image at the time of the beginning of the Church age. Modern Christian apologists argue frantically that Mary is in no way like Isis and Jesus is in no way similar to Horus, but it is very doubtful that early Christian worshipers did not recognize the similarity. As shown in Figure 5-1, the similarities in sacred art are undeniable. Claims like "Mary was never shown suckling Jesus" are not credible claims, they are attempts to distance two similar images, as in the example just mentioned.

Figure 5-1

So despite every attempt by the Church to destroy the divine feminine as shown in Mary, it failed at the time, and it continues to fail. During the reign of Pope John Paul the second there was some concern that he might declare Mary to be coequal to the trinity, which he was being pressured to do by many Roman Catholics. (Russell, 2000)

This was not a new idea however. While the Roman Church does not assert that Mary is coequal with God, or a coequal redeemer with Christ, it has a strong Marian theology that has asserted Mary as "Mother of God" since approximately 250 CE.[8] The Council of Ephesus formalized it as a dogma that Mary was the Mother of God in 431 CE, which also gives credence to the earlier foundations of the Marian position, as does the known veneration of Mary in Egypt, which began in the 200s. (Benz, 2009) Origen (c.185-c.253), one of the early Church fathers, refers to Mary as Theotokos, the "Mother of God" in his writings, as did other early Christians.

While many Protestants, particularly fundamentalists, deny any special significance to Mary, not only the Roman Catholic Church, but also the various branches of the Orthodox Church, the Coptic Church and even a plurality of Anglicans recognize her quasi-divine status, meaning that in terms of numbers, far more Christians venerate Mary than don't.

But of course, many other ancient goddesses were folded into the Church in one way or another. Some had their personalities folded into Mary. Others became saints, often by being commingled with Christian figures of surpassing devotion. A perfect example of the latter was Brig, or Brigid (called Brede or Bride in Scotland, and Brigantia in England). Brigid[9] was a mother goddess figure of pre-Christian Ireland. Part of the somewhat mysterious pantheon called the Tuatha Dé Danann.[10] She was a daughter of the chief of those gods, The Dagda. Brigid was a goddess of scholars, healers and poets. A solar goddess, she brought light to dark places, and inspiration to the most confused situations among the Celts.

Brigid was very popular among the people and the Church wanted to preserve her memory while helping the conversion of pagans in the Islands.

So, she was combined with a Saint, also given the name Brigid, Brigid of Kildare.[11] Brigid of Kildare, just as the goddess Brigid, had healing power, being particularly powerful in healing the blind. Brigid's Day, the sacred day of the goddess, became the Saint's day.[12] Brigid remained a Saint until 1969, when she was among the saints that were stripped of sainthood and expunged by Vatican II, based in large part on the undeniable fact that she was originally a pagan goddess.

Brigid is not the only ancient goddess transformed into a saint, either within the Roman tradition or elsewhere in the Christian world. The Greek goddess Aphrodite became Saint Aphrodite within the Orthodox Christian faith, as one of the Forty Virgin Martyrs from the 300s and revered for her steadfast service to Christ. The goddess Venus became the Catholic saint, Saint Venera, who is venerated as a martyr and whose power is believed to be over volcanoes.

To be clear, in general Christians fall into two camps on these goddess/saints. Among Orthodox, Catholic, and Anglican Christians, they are generally defended as being only incidentally connected to the goddesses from whom their legends descended, and complex stories are formulated and passed down to explain them - even though there is little to no evidence that the Christianized characters even existed.

For example, Saint Venera is said to have been born in Gaul on or about 100 AD and been martyred on July 26, 143 AD (Santa Venera, 2006). She is said to have killed a dragon, healed the sick and handled burning sulfur and oil without harm. She abolished a temple of Apollo with a prayer.

Even priests however admit that Venera as she is presented as a saint may never have existed at all, and that she may have been worshiped before Christian martyrs even existed (Paulist Fathers, 1915).

Among fundamentalist groups and some mainstream protestant denominations however, the Saints in general are either completely discarded, or bizarrely used in a futile attempt to prove that the Roman Church is actually of "the devil." In my years in the evangelical movement, in my late teens and early twenties, I heard truly ludicrous claims. Everything from "of course the canon of scripture already existed in 60 AD" (it did not) to the "Pope is the antiChrist," and worse. Of course, some of the same people told me that non-White people were the children of Ham and only had demons for souls. I quickly realized that I wanted nothing to do with them, and departed the movement,

In reality, religions emerge from one another, and Christianity and its offspring (Islam, Mormonism, etc.) are no exception, those newer faiths just don't like to admit it. Worship of the sacred feminine is, as we have seen, at least as old as, and probably older than, the sacred masculine - but Wicca says, accurately I think, that both are important and deserve honor and worship.

The survival of goddess worship through the most violent suppression of paganism in history is not some great and awe-inspiring evil plot, on the contrary, it is the strategy of an elderly mother whose child has turned violently against her. Luckily for those who profess the sacred feminine, it worked.

Of course this does not adequately mention Sophia (Wisdom) who was broadly worshiped within the early Christian faith, even before the Roman Church. Nor does it mention the fact that many Christians, including some fundamentalists, view the Holy Spirit as being "feminine." This is not a new view. Some Christians have viewed the Holy Spirit as female (and since it is part of trinity - therefore - a goddess) (van Oort, 2016), since very early in the history of the Church.

Section Two – The Modern Day
Chapter Five – Reemergence

Wicca, the New Age and related faiths are the fastest growing Spiritual path in the United States, Canada, and most of the Western World (Pagliarulo, 2022). How did that happen?

Arguably, Wicca (Craft of the Wise) and the Paganism of which it was part never completely vanished. It went underground. The vicious actions of the Church during the Inquisition, and of Islamic faith groups attempting to cleanse the areas of Europe under their control at around the same time, drove it into hiding. Paganism, particularly in the Scandinavian countries and Celtic, Welsh, Germanic and Saxon regions, endured, clandestinely. In Swedish churches for example, particularly in Gotland, preChristian picture stones, from the preexisting religions, were included in the buildings themselves. In a few cases, even being used as altars (Oehrl and Ljung, nd)

Was this to, in some way, preserve remnants of the old faiths? If so, it succeeded at some level and further at the very least, poems, epics, stories and oral traditions kept the ideas of the old gods and goddesses alive in the populace, even if they were no longer revered or worshiped in the churches.

Regardless, it began to reemerge into public view, like a flower that only blooms every so many years. In the 1940s and early 1950s, Gerald Gardner (1884–1964) publicly claimed to have been initiated into a secret witchcraft tradition that he called the "Old Religion" or "Wica." He began to publicize this tradition, which was influenced by ceremonial magic, folk magic, and other occult practices. Gardner's writings, such as *Witchcraft Today* (1954) and *The Meaning of Witchcraft* (1959), laid the foundational framework for Wicca. His teachings emphasized a duality of deities (the God and the Goddess - divine masculine and divine feminine), the importance of preserving nature, and ritual practices to drive the ceremonies that were to be performed.

He was joined by Doreen Valiente (1922-1999), who was a key figure in the early development of Wicca. She became Gardner's high priestess and a collaborator with him. She is credited with refining and revitalizing many of Gardner's rituals and writings. Valiente's contributions, including her *Witchcraft for Tomorrow* (1954), helped to shape Wiccan liturgy and ethics. Her work emphasized the importance of personal responsibility and the ethical principle of "An it harm none, do what ye will," which remains a central tenet of Wiccan practice.

After Gardner's initial popularization of Wicca, the religion began to spread and evolve. In the 1960s and 1970s, Wicca gained visibility and attracted followers, partially due to the rise of the countercultural movement and increased interest in alternative spiritualities, though other forces were also at play. Groups and covens began to form, and various branches of Wicca emerged. I call them "denominations of the faith of Wicca."

Raymond Buckland (1934–2009) was instrumental in bringing Wicca to the United States from the United Kingdom. In the 1960s, he introduced Gardnerian Wicca to America and wrote several influential books, including *Buckland's Complete Book of Witchcraft* (1986). His work helped to establish Wicca in the American cultural landscape and therefore contributed to its spread across North America.

As Wicca grew, new traditions began to emerge. Two major branches, or denominations if you prefer, as I do are

> M *Alexandrian Wicca:* Founded by Alexander and Maxine Sanders in the 1960s, Alexandrian Wicca shares many similarities with Gardnerian Wicca but includes additional elements of ceremonial magic.
>
> M *Feminist and Dianic Wicca*: In the 1970s, feminist witches, such as Zsuzsanna Budapest with her Dianic tradition, emphasized the worship of the Goddess and the feminist aspects of Wicca, while largely discarding the sacred masculine.

The late 20th century saw a broader revival of interest in various forms of paganism, including Wicca. The publication of influential works, such as *The Spiral Dance* by Starhawk (1979), helped to popularize Wiccan and feminist spiritualities. Organizations such as the Covenant of the Goddess, founded in 1975, also played a role in promoting Wiccan practices and community.In recent decades, Wicca has continued to diversify. Many practitioners now identify as eclectic Wiccans, combining elements from various traditions and sources to create personalized practices. The focus on nature, magic, and the duality of the divine remains central, but the ways in which these elements are interpreted and practiced can vary widely. If you think of it in more traditional terms, again, it's like denominations in Christianity. Ritual varies, practice varies, but the basic faith remains the same.

Wicca has increasingly gained legal and social recognition as the decades pass. In many countries, including the United States and parts of Europe, Wicca is recognized as a legitimate religion. This recognition has led to greater acceptance and understanding of Wiccan practices and beliefs. Legal recognition has permitted the formation of recognized, nonprofit organizations within the faith, including the Covenant of the Goddess, and other traditions. The SCOTUS has even ruled that practitioners of the faith may be buried in military cemeteries under the sign of their faith (generally an upright pentagram)

Wicca continues to adapt to modern challenges, including issues related to the environment, social justice, and ethical use of technology. The internet has facilitated the spread of Wiccan ideas and practices, allowing for a global exchange of knowledge and support among practitioners. There are foundations and charitable organizations with Wiccan roots, though I would agree that there are not yet enough of such organizations.

Modern Wicca, rooted in the works of Gerald Gardner and other early practitioners, has evolved significantly since its inception. From its origins in mid-20th century Britain, it has grown into a diverse and widespread spiritual movement. The continued development of Wicca reflects the dynamic nature of contemporary spirituality, with ongoing adaptations and reinterpretations to meet the needs of its practitioners.

Chapter Six - Wicca Today

While much of the mainstream media conflates Wiccans and Witches, as is pointed out by Jordan (2020) the two are not the same. There are Wiccans who are Witches, and there are Christians who are Witches, etc. Wicca is a religion, Witchcraft is a set of mystical practices. The two are not the same.

It is impossible to judge how many practicing witches there are in the United States, or in the world - but it is possible to estimate how many Wiccans there are. The religion is burgeoning.

In 1990 there were 8000 Wiccans in the US. In 2008 there were 340,000. This information is being drawn from the American Religious AmericanIdentification Survey, and Trinity College, full credit to them..

By 2014, there were ~1.3 million, according to the Pew Center for Religion, outstripping the Presbyterian church. In fact, if those figures are correct, which seems likely, the rate of growth for Wicca and associated neoPaganism is insanely high.

To calculate the rate of growth, we use the formula for the annual growth rate:

Growth Rate=(Final ValueInitial Value)1n−1\text{Growth Rate} = \left(\frac{\text{Final Value}}{\text{Initial Value}} \right)^{\frac{1}{n}} - 1

Where:

    M Final Value = 1,300,000 (value in 2014)

    M Initial Value = 340,000 (value in 2008)

    M nn = number of years between 2008 and 2014, which is 6 years.

Now, plugging in the values:

Growth Rate=(1,300,000340,000)16−1\text{Growth Rate} = \left(\frac{1,300,000}{340,000} \right)^{\frac{1}{6}} - 1 Growth

WHY WICCA

Rate=(3.8235)16−1\text{Growth Rate} = \left(3.8235 \right)^{\frac{1}{6}} - 1 Growth Rate≈1.2376−1\text{Growth Rate} \approx 1.2376 - 1 Growth Rate≈0.2376 or 23.76%\text{Growth Rate} \approx 0.2376 \text{ or } 23.76\%

The annual growth rate is approximately **23.76%**.

Let's put that in context. Islam, often "worried" about by some Christians, has an annual growth rate of ~1.5%. Atheism and "none" adherents have an annual growth rate of ~9.68% nationally. Wicca and neoPaganism appear to be blowing both out in terms of year over year growth.

Now of course, the argument from mainstream persons would be that such growth will inevitably stop. After all, traditional theologi‐

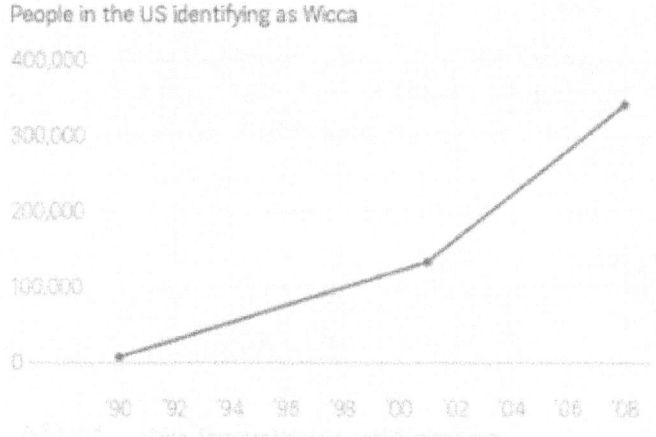

cal theory suggests that faith evolves, as mentioned before, from animism/spiritism to polytheism, possibly to henotheism, then to monotheism. Atheists then claim that the next step is from monotheism to atheism. For a large group of people, often quite well educated, to go backwards from monotheism to some combination of polytheism and animism/spiritism, runs against this wellworn theory and challenges its underlying assumptions.

That this is happening without active evangelization by the group with the over 20% growth rate is unthinkable to most uninvolved experts

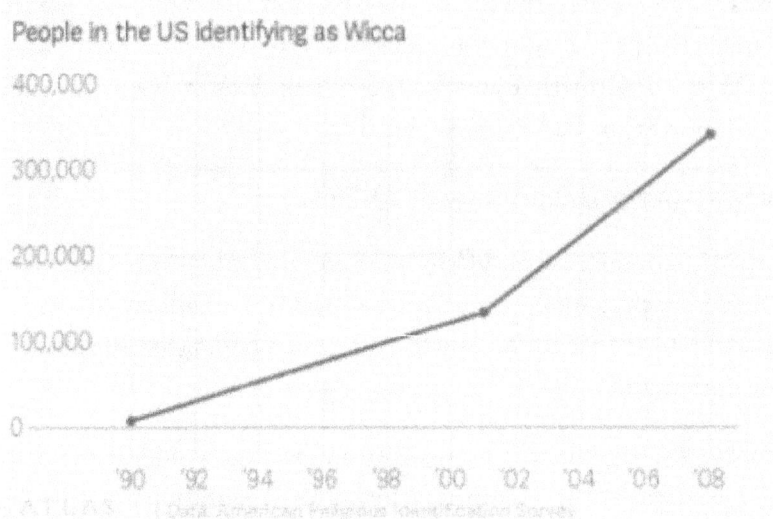

in theology and religion. Nevertheless, it is happening. Further, there is trong evidence that it will continue into the future. In a Yougov poll more than half of all Americans accepted some parts of the New Age, and a startling 17% listed Paganism among the things they accepted or believed in. Now Yougov polls are opt in, but they tend to be huge with many many tens of thousands of respondents, which lends some credibility to results. Nearly everything on this list is something that many Wiccans and neoPagans believe in, but that Paganism itself, which is viewed by many people as being "Wicca" has 17% interest shows the amount of growth that the Wiccan movement could and should still see.

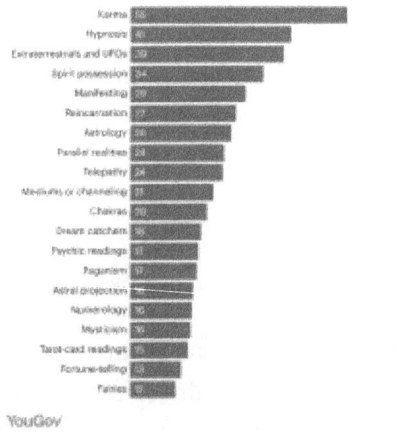

As the movement grows, it is worth looking at who is involved. Who are the Wiccans? Generally, they are just like everyone else. Pew suggests that they are similarly educated, and studies are just beginning on their political orientation. They tend to be openminded, and involved in other parts of the New Age movement.

Wicca is a diverse and inclusive tradition that varies in beliefs and practices from group to group, but remains centered around a deep respect for nature and a commitment to spiritual exploration. It is deeply ethical in general, and more open minded than not, with research indicating that while less politically involved than the average, Wiccans are generally liberals. (Marchetti, 2022)

There are within the Wiccan community two major strands. These two overarching families of traditions (denominations) are Initiatory and non-Initiatory. Let's take a look.

Families of Traditions

Initiatory Traditions

Initiatory traditions in Wicca refer to specific paths or practices within the religion where members undergo formal rituals of initiation to become recognized practitioners or members of a coven. These traditions often emphasize the passing of knowledge, spiritual growth, and a deeper connection to the mysteries of the Craft. Initiation is typically seen as a sacred and transformative process, marking an individual's entry into a more serious and committed practice of Wicca.

In initiatory Wicca, the process often involves:

1. **Coven-Based Initiation**: Many Wiccans follow an initiatory tradition where they join a coven (specifically a coven, very rarely a larger group) led by a High Priestess or High Priest or both. The coven provides structure, guidance, and community, and the

initiation serves as a way to pass on teachings that have been preserved through generations. This initiation may include rituals, oaths, and an acknowledgment of the responsibility that comes with practicing Wicca in a group setting.

2. **Degrees of Initiation**: Some Wiccan traditions have multiple degrees or levels of initiation. For example, in traditions like Gardnerian or Alexandrian Wicca, initiates progress through different stages—often starting as a "First Degree" initiate, then advancing to "Second" and "Third" Degrees. Each degree signifies a deeper understanding of the Craft and greater spiritual development. Higher degrees are typically associated with greater knowledge of rituals, magical practices, and the responsibilities of leadership within the coven.

3. **The Role of the Initiate**: During the initiation, individuals may be required to take oaths of secrecy and responsibility, as well as to affirm their commitment to the path. The experience is often described as deeply spiritual, symbolizing a rebirth or transformation. After initiation, the person is considered to have access to sacred knowledge and to be part of a lineage or tradition that connects them to the broader Wiccan community.

Non-Initiatory Traditions

Non-initiatory traditions in Wicca refer to practices and paths within the religion that do not require formal initiation by a coven or a higher authority. These traditions focus more on either individual practice, self-directed learning, and personal spiritual growth, or congregational worship under the leadership of priests and priestesses who may themselves have been initiated, but are ministering to a congregation primarily composed of what, in Christianity, would be called "pew-sitters." While non-initiatory traditions differ in their outlook on what is necessary to belong to the religion, they still embrace core Wiccan principles, such as reverence for nature, the worship of the God and Goddess, and obedience to the Wiccan Rede.

Here are some key characteristics of non-initiatory Wiccan traditions:

1. **Solitary Practice:** Many non-initiatory Wiccans prefer to practice alone, often referred to as "solitaries." These practitioners still follow traditional Wiccan rituals, honor the Sabbats and Esbats (the seasonal festivals and full moon rituals), and use divination and other sacred Wiccan practices, but they do so on their own, without the need for formal initiation or membership in a coven. Solitary Wiccans may create their own rituals, adapt teachings from various sources, and pursue a more personalized spiritual journey.
2. **Group Practice:** Other non-initiatory Wiccans practice in groups, often as large as many congregations in other faiths. The leaders in a given group often function as clergy in other religions, as well as being ritualists, arranging and leading the worship services, and also visiting the sick, attending to the needy as best they can, engaging in prison ministry, and otherwise acting as a spiritual leader of any faith. These groups are sometimes disparaged by initiatory Wiccans, but a reasonable amount of knowledge regarding the history of religion tells me that as Wicca continues to grow, this is likely to become the most common form. It provides community, spiritual leadership, and guidance at a level that is appropriate for families, and individuals with busy lives and little time.
3. **Eclectic Wicca:** Eclectic Wicca is a broad and flexible approach that allows individuals to pick and choose elements from various Wiccan traditions, as well as other spiritual or religious systems. Eclectic practitioners might blend rituals, beliefs, and practices to suit their own needs, preferences, and experiences. This path does not typically require initiation, or a group leader, and is more focused on personal spirituality and the freedom to adapt Wicca to one's unique circumstances.

These traditions form in many ways the natural evolution of faith. Small, private groups are the starting point for most faiths. House churches were there at the beginning of the Christian faith, and again with the Charismatic movement in the late 70s and 80s. Eventually however, the need to spiritually care for large numbers of people who were not interested in getting as deeply involved as the early members, led to a large, well organized Church, or churches. It seems likely to me that this will happen with Wicca too. Setting aside the question of how accurately it portrays earlier styles of Goddess worship, Wicca as we now see it, recently emerged, and is in the midst of what is probably its second major growth period. If the faith doesn't rise to the occasion, it is likely to fail.

The *Church of New Aeon* is Omnistic, but within it there are numerous Wiccan groups. The Church as a whole, as regards Wicca, takes the position that while there is an initiation procedure for priests and priestesses, there is room in congregations for "pew sitters" to come, be involved at the level that they can be, and help usher in the New Age for all people. A New Age of acceptance, peace, community, and hope.

Denominations

There are general divisions within Wicca (particularly writ large to include related faiths) and we have already mentioned some of them. In addition to the divisions, there are organized faith groups, both inside more established faiths, and independent of them, which I am calling denominations, particularly as some of them overlap established denominations that are not explicitly Wiccan.

Divisions

Let us take another look at the divisions, the general types that we are talking about: (a partial list)

> M **Alexandrian Wicca**: Introduced in 1967 –
>
>> " Focuses on the polarity of the god/goddess interaction in rituals. This often includes the "Great Rite" which mimes heterosexual intercourse

" Names for various entities vary from Gardnerian names for the same. Tools are less formalized and elements of Enochian magic and Qabalah are present.

" Alexandrian Wicca is very committed to an initiatory path for all new members.

" Considered part of Traditional British Wicca.

M **Central Valley Wicca**: Introduced in 1969

" A spinoff of Gardnerian Wicca with similar tools and similar practices. Centered in the Central Valley of California, introduced there by British expats, it very much resembles other British forms of Wicca.

" Considered part of traditional British Wicca

M **Algard Wicca**: Introduced in 1972

" Attempted Fusion of Alexandrian and Gardnerian Wicca

" Totally initiatory, you can only join by finding a group and being initiated

" Considered part of Traditional British Wicca.

M **Chthonioi Alexandrian Wicca**: Introduced in 1974

" Descended from Alexandrian Witchcraft

" Worships the Greco-Roman gods and goddesses

" Highly initiatory and primarily uses cross sex initiation (male to female/female to male)

M **Blue Star Wicca**: Introduced in 1975

" Based loosely on Alexandrian and Gardnerian Wicca

" Declares itself to be Great American Nontraditional Collective Eclectic Wicca.

" Uses music in its rituals

" Uses the Septagram as its holy symbol, not the Pentegram.

M **Feri Wicca:** Introduced in the 1950s and early 60s

" Described as an ecstatic not fertility based traditions

" Includes elements of many other traditions

" Uses the Septagram as its holy symbol, not the Pentegram

" Calls upon nature spirits, and the Faerie

M **Dianic Wicca**: Developed from the Women's Liberation Movement

" Female only

" Only worships the goddess

" Primarily transexclusionary, although more modern branches may not be.

M **Gardnerian Wicca:** Introduced in 1954 by Gerald Gardner

" Initiatory tradition

" Claims older roots, going back to hidden covens that survived the purges[13]

M **Seax Wica:** Introduced in 1973 by Raymond Buckland

WHY WICCA

" Non-initiatory tradition

" No secrecy oaths

" Allows for solitary worshippers to be considered part of the tradition

" Uses Woden and Freya as representations of the goddess and the god

" Is accepting of all people

Various other groups and traditions are numerous. Among those that I did not showcase above are:

M American Wicca (Open to all)

M Assembly of the Sacred Wheel (committed to social justice)

M Correllian Natavist Tradition

It is a safe statement to make that there are many ritual traditions in Wicca, even before you examine other neoPagan groups generally grouped with Wiccans, including Druids, Heathen[14] and so forth.

Denominations

Denominations are organizations within a religion. In Christianity, the denominations usually have at least slight differences in ritual or practice or doctrine. However, within, for example, the Anglican communion - one of the oldest Christian churches - there are high, low and broad church parishes. Among some other groups, like the Unitarians, neither doctrine or practice play much role, rather they are an association of people who worship in various ways, or in some cases, are atheists. Within Wicca there are also denominations as well as divisions. Some clear examples follow:

M Church of All Worlds – founded by Oberon and Morning Glory Zell-Ravenheart

M CUUPS (Covenant Unitarian Universalist Pagans)

M Feraferia

M Covenant of the Goddess (has hundreds of congregations)

M Church of Aphrodite (goddess only)

M Circle Sanctuary

M Aquarian Tabernacle Church (lots of resources)

M Correllian Natavist Church

M Church of the New Aeon (Order of Wicca)

Section 3 – Ritual Practice: solitary and group

Chapter Seven – Statements of Faith

The simple statement "an it harm none, do as ye will," is foundational to a much more complete statement of belief and practice called "The Wiccan Rede." The Rede is as follows, first in the short form, then in the long form.

Wiccan Rede (short form):

Bide the Wiccan Law ye must,

In perfect love and perfect trust.

Eight words the Wiccan Rede fulfill:

An' ye harm none, do what ye will.

What ye send forth comes back to thee

So ever mind the law of three[15].

Follow this with mind and heart,

Merry ye meet, and merry ye part.

Wiccan Rede (long form):

Bide the Wiccan Law ye must,

In Perfect Love and Perfect Trust;

Live ye must and let to live,

Fairly take and fairly give.

True in love, ever be,

Lest thy love be false to thee.

With a fool no season spend,

Nor be counted as his friend.

Soft of eye and light of touch,

Speak ye little, listen much.

Ever mind the rule of three,

What ye send out comes back to thee.

This lesson well, thou must learn

Ye only get what ye do earn.

Eight words the Wiccan Rede fulfill –

An it harm none, do as ye will.

Deosil go by waxing Moon,

Sing and dance the invoking Rune;

Widdershins go by waning Moon,

Chant ye then a freeing tune;

When the Lady's Moon is new,

Kiss thy hand to Her times two;

When the Bow rides in the eve

Turn to what you would achieve;

When the Moon rides at her peak,

Then thy heart's desire seek;

When the Sickle shows Her face

Release the old with proper grace.

Heed the North wind's mighty gale,

Lock the door & trim the sail;

When the wind comes from the South,

Love will kiss thee on the mouth;

When the wind blows from the West,

Hearts will find their peace and rest;

When the wind blows from the East,

Expect the new and set the feast.

Nine woods in the Cauldron go,

Burn them quick and burn them slow;

Grape and fir and apple tree,

And Hawthorn are sacred to Thee,

Willow, hazel, rowan, birch,

And oak will guide your every search;

Elder be the Lady's tree –

Burn it not or cursed ye'll be.

Birchwood in the fire goes

To tell us true what Goddess knows.

Oak trees tower great with might,

Burn the Oak for God's insight.

Rowan is a tree of power

Causing life and magick flower.

Willows at the waters stand

To help us to the Summerland.

Hawthorn burn to purify

And draw the faerie to your eye.

Hazel tree, the wisdom sage,

Lends strength that comes with honoured age.

White the flowers of Apple tree,

The holy gift, fecundity.

Grape grows upon the fruitful vine,

Sacred gifts of joy and wine.

Fir's ever greenness declares life

Succeeds beyond any strife.

Heed ye flower, bush, and tree,

And by the Lady Blessed be.

Where the rippling waters flow

Cast a stone and truth ye'll know;

Four times the Major Sabbats mark

In the light and in the dark:

As the old year dies again

The new begins at dark Samhain.

When flowers blossom through the snow

Fair Brighid casts her seed to sow.

When winter yields to warmth's return Let the Beltane fires burn.

As summer turns to Lammas night

First fruits and Grain Gods reach their height.

Four times the Minor Sabbats fall

Use the Sun to mark them all:

At Yuletide, with feast and mirth

We celebrate the God Child's birth.

Spring Equinox, Eostara's fest,

All newborn creatures will be blessed.

When the Sun has reached its height

Celebrate the greatest Light.

Offer thanks at second reaping;

Mabon poised for winter's keeping.

Cast the circle thrice about,

To keep unwelcome spirits out.

To bind the spell well every time,

Let the spell be spake in rhyme.

Follow this with mind & art,

Bright the cheeks and warm the heart,

And merry meet & merry part

And merry meet again!

Obviously the long form of the Rede is much more complete. In Christian terms it might be considered to be a combination of the ten commandments, the Nicene Creed, a listing of holidays and very basic guidance on ceremony. It covers morality, doctrine, which is sparse throughout Wicca, the calendar of the year with its holy days, and what is being celebrated at each one.

Some argue that this is simply not a complex enough statement of faith, but it really does cover everything, leaving room for personal spirituality and seeking. It even has a reference to the Summerlands, which many Wiccans believe is our ultimate goal for a life well lived.

Even the short form is a powerful statement of both faith and morality. Often recited in some group worship sessions as part of the ritual, it clearly points out the advantages of doing good and the potential danger of doing ill to others. It reinforces the benevolent nature of Wicca generally and encourages what is called "the Right Hand Path" - the path of light and goodness.

Let's consider a few of these lines:

Bide the Wiccan Law ye must,

In perfect love and perfect trust.

This line calls for adherence to the "Wiccan Law," which centers on the principles of love, trust, and respect. The phrase "perfect love and perfect trust" reflects the balance and harmonious relationships between practitioners, the divine, and all living things. It suggests that in order to live a worthwhile life, one must cultivate unconditional love and trust in oneself, others, and the divine forces.

This of course closely resembles many calls in Christianity and other faiths for love, harmony, trust, and good treatment of others.

Live and let live, fairly take and fairly give.

This teaches the values of equality, fairness, and reciprocity. It emphasizes that life should be lived with respect for others' autonomy, rights, and well-being. To "fairly take" suggests not exploiting others, while "fairly give" indicates generosity and balance in all relationships. It reinforces the concept of mutual respect and harmony.

Cast the Circle thrice about, to keep the evil spirits out.

Casting the circle is a common practice in Wiccan ritual to create sacred space and protect against negative influences. This line reflects the importance of boundary-setting in one's spiritual practices and the need to guard oneself and the space from harmful energies or entities.

Forms of this are seen in other faiths. The circumambulation of the altar by the priest in many traditions is a remnant reminder of this practice, which has been incorporated into many forms of Christianity over time. Likewise in some cases the entire church may be circled, often three times, by the priest, acolytes and so forth. This is a creation of sacred space, even if it is no longer remembered exactly as such.

Soft of eye and light of touch, speak little, listen much.

These words encourage Wiccans to be observant, sensitive, and mindful. "Soft of eye" refers to the ability to perceive with an open heart, not judging or rushing to conclusions. "Light of touch" implies gentleness in both physical and emotional actions. "Speak little, listen much" emphasizes the importance of listening more than speaking, cultivating wisdom, humility, and understanding.

Again, you can see echoes of this in other faiths. There are many scriptures in the Christian Bible, for example, that urge gentleness (a soft answer turns away wrath is but one). Today's Christians have, in large part, forgotten the faith, or turned it to suit their own desires, but Christ himself, according to the scriptures, when Simon Peter cut off a man's ear attempting to defend Christ, told Simon Peter and all his followers to put away their swords.

Honor the Old Ones in deed and in truth. Honor the Earth our Mother, and honor the Starry Sky our Father. Honor the creatures of the Earth, and the spirits of the sea and sky.

These lines are doctrinal. They lay out respect, honor, and reverence to the "Old Ones" - the goddesses, gods, and ancestral spirits that are reverenced in Wicca. Honor the cosmos, including Gaia, the earth mother. Honor the creatures of Gaia, on the earth, in the sea, and in the air. Direct, simple, religious commandments.

By the sacred laws of three, three times what thou send'st out must be.

This refers to the "Law of Threefold Return," which is the Wiccan belief that any energy (whether positive or negative) you send out into the world returns to you three times over. This line encourages Wiccans to be mindful of their actions and intentions, ensuring they contribute positively to the world, knowing that their energy will return to them magnified.

Other faiths call this type of thing Karma, but Wicca is very specific in that there is an expectation that the good you do, and the bad, will be returned to you three times over. This is particularly true for the practitioner who knows they are doing good or ill, but also true for the one who does such things by their nature and not from any spiritual desire.

Follow this with mind and heart, merry ye meet, merry ye part.

This closing speaks to the joyful and positive nature of Wiccan practice. It suggests that Wiccans should approach their spiritual and community lives with a positive attitude, staying connected with love and light. The phrase "merry ye meet, merry ye part" expresses the importance of leaving every interaction in a state of goodwill and joy, whether in ritual, community, or daily life.

I find this particularly amazing as an outlook, given the prejudice that those who practice Wicca and its predecessors have faced. Yet, the faith is a positive one that looks forward with joy. Much is to be said for that.

Each stanza offers guidelines for living with integrity, compassion, and balance. The Rede emphasizes respect for all living beings, the Earth, and the divine forces that shape the world. It asks practitioners to take personal responsibility for their actions and to live with a sense of fairness, respect, and reciprocity.

Many lines in the Rede stress the importance of balance—between self and others, nature and the cosmos, thought and action. Wicca's ethical framework teaches practitioners to live in harmony with all aspects of life and the universe.

The Rede also reinforces the importance of ritual and conscious spiritual practice. It asks Wiccans to act with intention, respect the sacredness of space and time, and approach their magic (the Wiccan form of prayer) with caution and awareness.

The Rede encourages personal development, humility, and learning through listening. It invites Wiccans to cultivate wisdom and to honor the ancestors and the divine through truth and action.

In summary, the Wiccan Rede, in its extended form, is a comprehensive guide for living an ethical and balanced life. Its functional meaning is about acting responsibly, cultivating love and respect, and understanding the interconnectedness of all beings. Practitioners are called to be mindful of their actions and to live in harmony with nature, others, and the divine, while maintaining a deep sense of personal and collective responsibility.

Chapter Eight – Holy Days, the Great Wheel

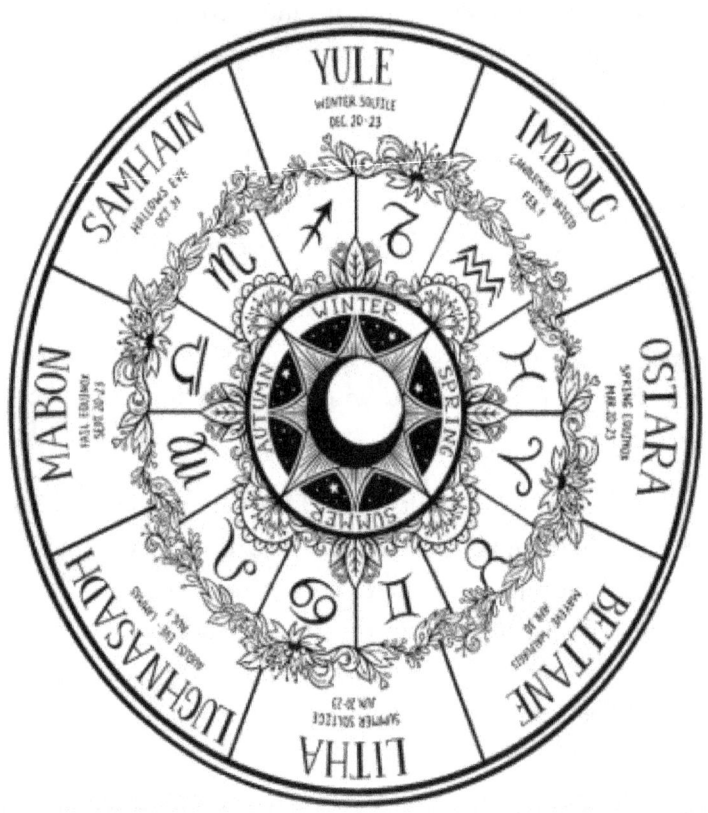

In Wicca, the **Wheel of the Year** is a cycle of eight holy days or Sabbats, each marking a point of seasonal change and honoring the cycles of nature, the Earth, and the divine. These Sabbats are celebrated in alignment with the solstices, equinoxes, and the midpoints between them. They represent the agricultural cycle (very important to the precursor faiths and to some modern practitioners), the phases of the Goddess (from Maiden to Mother to Crone), and the balance of light and dark in the world.

Some traditions also include the cyclical defeat of the Oak King, who is the ruler of the summer, of light, fertility and growth by the Holly King, who is the ruler of winter, darkness and death, and who then, in his turn, is replaced again by the Oak King as spring comes again.

The general premise of these holy days is largely universal. Nearly all historic cultures after agriculture began had a harvest festival, a midwinter festival, a spring festival, etc. Wicca brings together the solstices and the quinoxes, giving each its own celebration.

In the northern hemisphere, particularly as you get further from the equator, the vital importance of the festivals to premodern people becomes stronger and stronger. Without modern markets and supply chains, it was important for each village to have sufficient stores by the end of summer, to survive the winter. Thus, the celebrations were about fertility, growth, harvest and preparation for the cold and dark. Even with the most successful preparation and storage of food, the winter was replete with death, particularly of elders.

These eight festivals, or "sabbats" are the liturgical center of Wicca. They distill the festivals that came before the modern day. They continue to celebrate the earth, and its abundance, and the seasons, including those that are most dangerous (still) for the people. Celebrating them is basic to the faith.

Generally, the Wiccan New Year is viewed as being **Samhain** (pronounced Soween). Samhain is the final harvest festival of the year, it occurs on October 31/November 1, and is concurrent with the modern holiday of Halloween.

Samhain marks the end of the harvest and the beginning of winter. It is a time to honor ancestors and loved ones who have passed. The veil between the physical world and the spirit world is believed to be thinnest during **Samhain**, making it an ideal time for divination and connecting with those on the other side. It is also a celebration of transformation, death, and rebirth, symbolizing the death of the old year and the birth of the new.

Yule is the longest night and the shortest day of the year, representing the triumph of light over darkness. This Sabbat celebrates the rebirth of the Sun, symbolized by the birth of the God (often depicted as the "New Sun" or

"Infant Sun"). It's a time of renewal, hope, and the return of light. Traditions of gift-giving, feasts, and decorating evergreen trees are associated with this Sabbat, celebrating life, growth, and warmth.

For those who follow the progress of the Oak King and the Holly King - it is here that the Oak King puts the Holly King to flight, as light begins to return to the world with lengthening days. In those lengthening days, the Oak King rules.

While **Yule** was a specific midwinter celebration, the name of which has come forward into Wicca, nearly all cultures had one. The themes of the birth of a god, or the God, and the return of the sun existed far and wide. In Christianity, Christmas took the place of the midwinter festival and was placed on the date of Saturnalia - a Roman version of midwinter. In Hinduism, Makar Sankranti, also known in some regions as Lohri is, while a few days later, their midwinter festival. In China Dong Zhi is celebrated (and incidentally, it is the day when all Chinese count themselves as a year older). It is impossible to estimate exactly how many versions of midwinter there are, and important to remember that in the southern hemisphere it is celebrated in June, but it is largely universal as a holiday.

Imbolc marks the midpoint between the Winter Solstice and the Spring Equinox. It is a time of purification, cleaning, and preparing for the new growth of spring. The Goddess is often honored in her aspect as Brigid, the deity of fire, fertility, poetry, and healing (who as we mentioned before was "absorbed" into Christianity as Saint Brigid). It is a time to light candles, perform cleansing rituals, and plant the seeds (both literally and metaphorically) for new beginnings. Imbolc is also connected to the awakening of the Earth from its winter slumber.

Ostara celebrates the balance of light and dark, as day and night are equal in length. This Sabbat is focused on fertility, new beginnings, and the awakening of life after the winter months. It is a time to plant physical seeds in the ground, as well as metaphorical seeds for personal growth and new projects. Symbols of Ostara include eggs (representing fertility and new life) and rabbits (representing fertility). It is a time to celebrate balance, harmony, and the blossoming of new possibilities.

Interestingly, **Ostara** is arguably, the origin of Easter. The goddess Eostre is the namesake of the Easter holiday. She is depicted as a goddess of fertility, spring, flowers, rebirth, and the dawn. The word "Easter" comes from her name. Eostre's name itself comes from the Old English word Ēosturmōnaþ, which means "Month of Ēostre." The monk Bede is the primary source for knowledge of the worship of Eostre, but it is very likely that she was a tribal goddess in the area. (Winnick, 2016) It is certainly true that the holiday of Easter as we know it now draws heavily from pagan influences, as well as Christian religious ones.

Beltane is a fire festival celebrating fertility, passion, and the union of the Goddess and God. It marks the start of the fertile growing season, a time to celebrate life, love, and creativity. The Maypole dance is a traditional Beltane activity, symbolizing the union of the Divine masculine and feminine. It is a time for rituals of manifestation, creativity, and love, as well as honoring physical and sexual energy. **Beltane** invites practitioners to connect with their creative power and life force.

Litha (midsummer, summer solstice) celebrates the height of summer, the longest day and shortest night of the year. It is a time to honor the Sun at the peak of its power, representing vitality, energy, and growth. The Sabbat is focused on the celebration of light, abundance, and the culmination of growth. Litha is a time to celebrate the fullness of life, and the power of the Sun, often associated with the God in his aspect as the powerful and vibrant Horned God. It is also a time for divination and magic.

For those whose practice includes the Oak King and the Holly King, it is at this time, often with a ritual battle, that the Holly King takes charge for the next few months, as the light wanes.

Lammas (Lughnasadh) marks the first of the three harvest festivals, specifically focused on the grain harvest. It is a time of thanksgiving for the abundance of the Earth and a time to reflect on the sacrifices that are part of the cycle of life. The Sabbat emphasizes the importance of giving thanks for what has been provided, and it is a time of sharing the fruits of one's labors. *Lammas* is also about reflection and preparing for the coming of the darker months ahead.

Mabon is the second of the harvest festivals, and it marks the Autumn Equinox, a time when day and night are again in balance. It is a time to give thanks for the harvest and the abundance of the Earth, but also to prepare for the coming winter. *Mabon* is a time of reflection, balance, and gratitude, as well as honoring the balance between the light and the dark. It is a time to prepare for the darker half of the year and reflect on what has been accomplished. The Sabbat is associated with the idea of reaping what one has sown and making plans for the future.

In addition to these eight sabbats that dominate the religious calendar of Wicca, there are also esbats. Ceremonies that some Wiccans use to celebrate either full, or new, or both, moons. Sometimes called the second wheel of the year, or the lesser wheel, there are thirteen lunar cycles per year, and depending on the group or if solitary one's personal practice, they may be celebrated either on the full moons or the new moons, or as mentioned, in some cases, both.

Chapter Nine – Rituals and Ritual Practice

Alright, so let's lay out a basic ritual, and go through the various steps in that ritual to discuss it in more depth and detail.

Basic Ritual Structure

1. Establish the intention of the ritual.

2. Construct ritual outline.

3. Purify self and ritual space

4. Set up altar

5. Cast the circle

6. Call the quarters

7. Invoke higher forces (God, Goddess, Over Soul, All That Is)

8. Raise energy (chant, sing, dance, sex, meditation, etc.)

9. Ritual observance

10. Perform magical workings

11. Release the energy towards it's purpose.

12. Thanksgiving (Cakes and Ale).

13. Earth any residual energy and ground yourself

14. Thank higher forces

15. Close the Circle.

16. Clean up altar.

Detail –

1. Establish the intention of the ritual –

a. **Clarity of Purpose**

Explanation: Before beginning any ritual, it's essential to be clear about your purpose. This can be an emotional, physical, or spiritual goal. Your intention should be specific and well-defined. A vague or general intention (e.g., "I want to be happier") is less likely to yield effective results than a more focused one (e.g., "I seek healing from past emotional pain" or "I wish to manifest abundance in my career").

Example: If you are performing a ritual for protection, your intention might be, "I am seeking protection from negative energies and harmful influences."

b. **Formulating the Intention**

Explanation: Formulating your intention involves stating it clearly and directly. Some Wiccans may use specific words or phrases, while others prefer a more open, meditative approach. It's important that the intention feels authentic and resonates deeply with the practitioner. Whether spoken aloud, thought internally, or written down, the intention should align with your spiritual or material desires.

Example: A spoken affirmation could be, "I call upon the powers of the elements and the divine to assist me in manifesting prosperity and well-being in my life."

c. **Visualization of the Outcome**

Explanation: Visualization is a powerful tool for setting intention in Wiccan ritual. Once the intention is clear, practitioners often engage in a process of visualization — imagining the desired outcome vividly. This strengthens the focus on the intention and helps direct the ritual's energy.

Example: If the intention is for healing, a practitioner might visualize light or energy flowing into their body, filling them with health and vitality.

d. **Aligning with the Elements and Energies**

Explanation: In Wicca, rituals often involve invoking the four elements (Earth, Air, Fire, Water) or the energies of the God and Goddess. Practitioners align their intention with these elements to amplify the ritual's power. Each element corresponds to different aspects of life (e.g., Earth for stability, Water for emotions, Fire for passion, and Air for intellect or communication).

Example: During a ritual for clarity or communication, a Wiccan might focus on the element of Air, perhaps lighting incense or waving a feather to connect with the energy of thought and intellect, aligning the ritual's intention with that element.

1. Construct the ritual outline –

a. We have set the ritual intention already. So that is done.
b. We must determine that we have the tools we may need. Some practitioners will say that you can use anything - a blade of grass for an athame, a paper cup, whatever - and perhaps for some that is true. However, focus is essential, will is essential and focusing will is basic. It is easier to focus will with ritual tools that have been consecrated and prepared for use, in my personal opinion. Tools might include the following:
    i. **Athame** (ritual knife)
    ii. **Wand** (to direct energy)
    iii. **Candles** (representing the elements or deities)

      iv. **Chalice** (often for offerings, drink, or blessings)
      v. **Cauldron** (for transformation or burning items)
      vi. **Incense** (for spiritual clarity)
      vii. **Altar** (where tools and offerings are placed)
  c. Other tools might, depending on the flavor of your belief system include crystals, herbs, oil, offerings (such as food, flowers, or other symbolic items), a bell, a sword, or anything tied specifically to your intention.

3. Purify self and ritual space –

Purifying the self ensures that your energy is clear and focused before engaging in ritual. Different techniques are used. If you are performing a ritual alone you should choose the one or ones that are most useful to you.

a. Meditation and Grounding:

> **M** Meditation helps calm the mind, clear distractions, and align with your higher self and the divine. A simple practice is to sit in silence, focus on your breath, and clear your mind of any thoughts.
>
> **M Grounding** involves connecting your energy to the Earth. A common technique is to imagine roots growing from your feet deep into the Earth, absorbing stability and releasing any negative energy.
>
> **M** Cleansing Baths: A ritual bath using herbs, salts, and essential oils is a powerful way to purify and ground the body and energy. Common ingredients include **sea salt** (for purification), **lavender** (for calm and protection), **rosemary** (for clearing negativity), and **sage** (for spiritual cleansing). You can prepare a bath by adding these ingredients to warm water and soaking in it while visualizing negative energies being washed away.

b. Breathwork and Visualization:

WHY WICCA

M Breathwork can be used to cleanse your energy. Inhale deeply, imagining positive energy filling you, and exhale while visualizing negativity leaving your body.

M **Visualization** can be a tool for self-purification. Imagine a bright light (often white or golden) surrounding you, filling your aura and pushing away any unwanted energies.

c. Purifying the ritual Space:

M Smudging is one of the most popular methods for cleansing a ritual space. You can use **sage**, **palo santo**, **cedar**, or even **sweetgrass**. Light the herb bundle and walk around the space, letting the smoke fill every corner while focusing on clearing away any unwanted or stagnant energies. Thus, preparing the space for the ritual to come.[16]

4. Set up the altar

This presumes you do not have a permanent ritual space where you maintain an altar. If that is correct, then after purifying yourself and the ritual space, set up your altar. What follows is a guide, including a simple diagram to show what the altar might look like:

Choose Your Space:

M Select a quiet, clean space where you can focus. It could be a table, a cloth spread on the floor, or any flat surface.

M Ideally, it should be away from distractions and in a place where you feel comfortable.

Cleanse the Space:

M Before setting up your altar, it's good practice to purify the space using techniques like smudging or salt, possibly with visualization (as discussed previously).

Set the Altar Cloth:

M Place a cloth on the surface of your altar. The cloth can be any color, but commonly used colors in Wicca are **white** (purity), **red** (passion), **green** (growth), or **purple** (spirituality).

M This cloth symbolizes the sacredness of the space and provides a foundation for your altar tools.

Place the Altar Tools:

M Candles: Typically, a **white candle** (representing the Goddess or spirit) is placed in the center. Another common use of candles is silver for the Goddess and gold for the God. If you want to honor other specific deities, you can place candles in colors that correspond to those deities or elements.

M **Incense:** Light incense to purify the space and connect with the element of air. Frankincense, lavender, or sage are common choices.

M **Athame (or Ritual Knife):** If you are using an athame for your ritual, place it on the altar, usually near the back right of the altar (if you are facing it). It represents the element of fire and the masculine energy.

M **Chalice:** A **chalice** or cup can be placed on the altar to represent the element of water and the feminine energy. It can hold wine, water, or any liquid corresponding to your ritual needs.

M **Pentacle:** A **pentacle** (or another sacred symbol) can be placed at the center of your altar or toward the back, symbolizing the element of earth and balance.

M **Crystals:** If you're working with specific energy or intentions, you can place crystals such as **clear quartz** (for clarity), **amethyst** (for spiritual connection), or **black tourmaline** (for protection).

M **Deity Symbols or Images:** If you honor specific deities, you can place their symbols, representations, or statues on the altar. For example, a statue of the God and Goddess can be placed on either side.

M **Herbs/Flowers:** If relevant to the ritual, you can add herbs or flowers that correspond to your intention. For example, **roses** for love, **lavender** for calm, or **sage** for cleansing.

M **Elemental Tools:** You can place small items representing the elements, like a bowl of salt (earth), a bell or feather (air), a candle (fire), and a dish of water (water).

Simple temporary altar setup as an

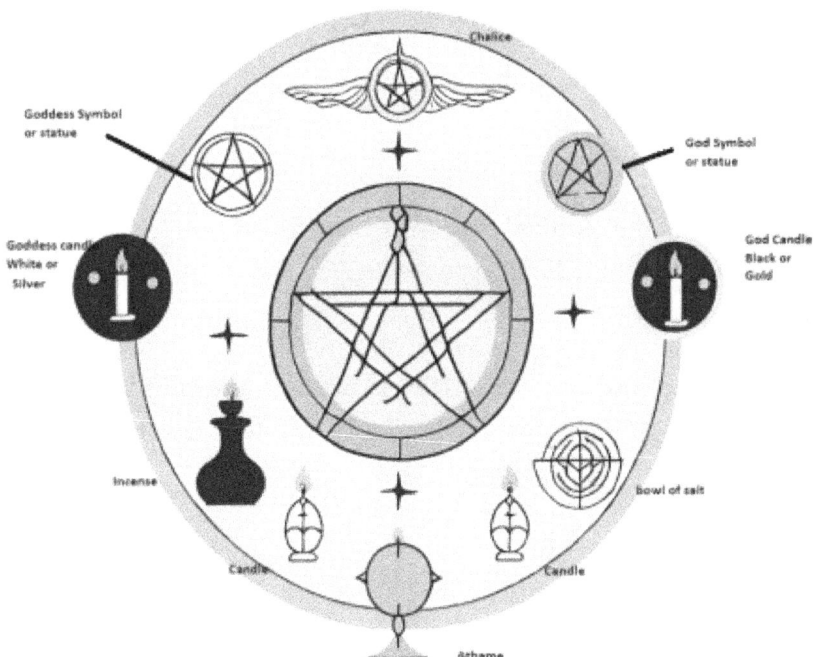

example

[17]

5/6/7. Casting the Circle, calling the quarters and invoking the deities –

Center Yourself:

⋈ Take a few moments to **ground** and **center** yourself. This can be done by breathing deeply and focusing your energy inward.

⋈ Some Wiccans like to meditate for a few minutes to calm their minds and clear any distractions.

Set Your Intention:

⋈ Set the clear intention which you developed in Step 1 for your ritual working. This can be a simple affirmation or visualization of what you hope to achieve during the circle.

⋈ You may also wish to **invoke** deities or energies you are working with at this point, such as the God and Goddess, the four elements, or specific spirits.

Visualize the Circle:

⋈ Stand in the center of your chosen space and imagine a sphere of white or golden light surrounding you. This light can expand outward until it forms a circle around you.

⋈ As you visualize the circle, imagine it growing stronger, solidifying, and becoming impenetrable, protecting you and the space within from negative energies.

Use a Tool to Cast the Circle:

⋈ Athame (ritual knife): If you are using an athame (a ritual knife), hold it in your dominant hand and trace a circle in the air. Some practitioners will move around the space in a clockwise or deosil direction (following the path of the sun) to visualize the circle's boundary.

WHY WICCA

M **Wand:** If you don't use an athame, you can cast the circle with a wand. Simply point it forward and begin tracing the circle around yourself.

M **Direction of Movement:** Move **clockwise (deosil)** for invoking energy, blessings, and spiritual work. This is a common direction for most rituals. **Counterclockwise (widdershins)** is typically used for banishing or protection work, though this is a personal choice.

Invoke the Elements (Call the Quarters):

M As you move around the circle, most Wiccans choose to **invoke the elements** to further empower the space and enhance the circle's protective properties. You can represent the elements as follows:

" **East (Air):** Place your hand or tool toward the east and say something like, "I call upon the element of Air, to aid me in this working.[18]"

" **South (Fire):** Place your hand or tool toward the south and say, "I call upon the element of Fire, to aid me in this working."

" **West (Water):** Place your hand or tool toward the west and say, "I call upon the element of Water, to aid me in this working."

" **North (Earth):** Place your hand or tool toward the north and say, "I call upon the element of Earth, to aid me in this working."

M As you invoke the elements, visualize their energies filling the space and strengthening the circle.

Create the Protective Barrier:

M Once the circle is cast, you may choose to **seal** the circle by visualizing the light around it becoming impenetrable, or you can physically "draw" a protective line by walking along the perimeter or using a symbolic gesture such as raising the athame or wand.

M Some practitioners also visualize the circle becoming a **dome** or a **bubble** of energy, which can protect against outside influences during the ritual.

Invocation of Deities or Spirits:

M If your ritual involves calling on deities, spirits, or guides, this is the time to invite them into your circle. You may say something like:

" "I call upon the God and Goddess to join me in this sacred space."

" "I invite my ancestors/spirits/guides to be with me during this time."

M It's essential to acknowledge these energies with respect and reverence.

8, 10, and 11. Raise energy (this is the equivalent of prayer in Judeo-Christian faiths):

There are a number of ways that energy is raised, ranging from invocations - which are effectively prayers with a stronger intention, to singing to breathing. What a particular ritual uses varies whether it is solitary or group, and is also dependent to a degree on the intention that we set, way back in step 1.

Chanting or Invocations

M Purpose: Chanting, singing, or invoking deities serves to build rhythm, create vibration, and raise energy.

ℳ **Method**: Repeating words of power or specific invocations during rituals helps lift the energy of the group or individual. The chanting can be rhythmic, deepening the trance state and raising the emotional and energetic charge of the ritual.

Dancing or Movement

ℳ Purpose: Movement stimulates the flow of energy throughout the body and the ritual space.

ℳ **Method**: Dancing, drumming, or even simple ritual movements such as circling or jumping can raise energy. The energetic output can be increased by the speed and intensity of the movement, helping to focus energy toward the desired goal.

Drumming or Musical Instruments

ℳ Purpose: The vibrations from drumming or other instruments can elevate the energy and help practitioners enter a trance state.

ℳ **Method**: Rhythmic drumming or sound vibrations stimulate the body and mind, raising both individual and group energy. The sound helps synchronize the practitioners, raising their collective power.

Breathing Techniques

ℳ Purpose: Breath is considered a vital source of energy in Wiccan rituals, and conscious breathing can help control and direct energy.

ℳ **Method**: Practitioners may use deep breathing, breath control, or specific breathing exercises (such as "the breath of fire") to move energy through their body and focus it into a specific purpose or direction.

The Elements

M Purpose: The four elements (Earth, Air, Fire, and Water) represent different energies that can be invoked and utilized in rituals.

M **Method**: Each element has a unique energy. For example:

" **Earth** can be used for grounding and stability.

" **Air** for mental clarity and inspiration.

" **Fire** for transformation and passion.

" **Water** for healing and emotion.

M Wiccans may invoke these elements through the use of additional elemental tools (e.g., candles, incense, salt, and water) and direct the energy as needed.

Candle Magic and Flames

M Purpose: Candles represent the element of Fire and are used to focus and amplify it's energy.

M **Method**: Candle flames can serve as a focal point for concentrating intent. The color of the candle may correspond to the purpose of the ritual (e.g., green for prosperity, red for passion, blue for protection). Gazing at the flame while concentrating on the desired outcome helps raise the energy.

Group Energy (If in a Congregation or Group)

M Purpose: In a group ritual, energy is amplified as the participants focus on a common intent.

M **Method**: Energy raised by multiple people is often much more potent than that of a single person. Group members can synchronize their movements, breathing, and chants to create a shared energetic field, raising the collective "cone of power[19]" in the circle.

The Power of Intention

M Purpose: Ultimately, the energy raised is directed by the will and intention of the practitioner(s).

M **Method**: Intent is a critical component in Wicca. Focused intent (will) is what gives energy its direction and purpose. Through concentration, visualization, and emotional engagement, practitioners can amplify the energy raised toward their specific goals.

9. Ritual observance: For a solitary practitioner of the faith, this is a matter of personal taste[20] but in a group setting, the decisions should be made either by the celebrants (high priestess and/or high priest) or by community members through discussion and consensus. Possible ritual observance for groups are things like:

Offering or Sacrifice to Deities

M Purpose: To honor and give thanks to deities, spirits, or nature for their guidance or blessings.

M **Method**: Offerings can take many forms, such as:

" Lighting candles or incense to honor specific deities during the ritual.

" Offering food, drink, or flowers on an altar or sacred space.

" Making symbolic offerings, like pouring water or wine into a vessel for the gods, or burning herbs or incense.

" Some practitioners also perform a gesture of gratitude, such as bowing or kneeling to specific deities or to their own patrons.

Meditation or Silent Reflection

M Purpose: To internalize the energy raised, reflect on the ritual's meaning, and connect deeply with any insights or messages from the divine or spirit worlds.

M **Method**: After a ritual, practitioners may enter a period of quiet meditation to allow the energy to settle and listen for any spiritual guidance, intuition, or divine messages. This could involve:

" Sitting quietly with closed eyes.

" Focusing on a particular object or symbol of the ritual.

" Asking for clarity or insight regarding the intention of the ritual.

Journaling or Recording the Experience

M Purpose: To document the energy raised, thoughts, and any outcomes from the ritual, and track progress in magical workings or spiritual development.

M **Method**: Many Wiccans keep a Book of Shadows or a magical diary where they write down:

" The intention or purpose of the ritual.

" The methods and tools used during the ritual.

" Any insights, messages, or feelings experienced.

" Results or progress related to the spell or working.

" This helps to build a connection with their magical practices and observe patterns over time.

12. Thanksgiving - Cakes and Ale.

Symbolism of Cakes and Ale in Wicca

The "Cakes and Ale" are symbolic offerings that represent several key themes in Wicca:

- **The Sacredness of the Earth**: The cakes, often made from simple grains such as wheat, and the ale (or sometimes wine) symbolize the fruits of the Earth. They are seen as offerings to the Earth itself, acknowledging its fertility and abundance. In this context, they represent the cycle of life, death, and rebirth—the fundamental aspects of nature that Wicca celebrates.

- **Balance of the Feminine and Masculine**: The food and drink represent both the masculine and feminine energies. In many traditions, the **cakes** (especially if they are bread or grain-based) represent the **feminine** or **Earth**, as grains are traditionally associated with fertility and growth. The **ale or wine**, on the other hand, is often seen as symbolizing the **masculine**, as it involves fermentation and transformation, processes that are often linked to the masculine principle. Together, these elements represent the sacred union of opposites, which is a major theme in most Wiccan worship.

- **Celebration and Gratitude**: Cakes and ale are also a way to offer thanks to the deities, spirits, and the elements for their participation in the rite. The act of sharing food and drink fosters a sense of community and reinforces the interconnectedness of all participants.

- **The Circle of Life**: Wicca is deeply rooted in the idea of cycles—life, death, and rebirth, reflected in the cycles of the Moon, the seasons, and the Wheel of the Year. Cakes and ale embody this idea, as they are food and drink that sustain the body, just as the Earth sustains life.

The Ritual Process of Cakes and Ale

The "Cakes and Ale" portion of the ritual typically comes at the end of the ritual, after the invocations are complete and the energy raised has been directed. It serves as both a closing and a grounding activity, reinforcing the ritual's intentions and celebrating the bond between the group members, the divine, and the natural world.

a. The Preparation

M **Cakes**: The cakes are usually made from simple, natural ingredients, typically **wheat** or **flour**, although other grains such as barley or oats may also be used. These represent the Earth's bounty and are often round, symbolizing completeness and the cycle of life. In some circles, the cakes may be homemade by a member and brought to the ritual as an offering.

The cakes are often **blessed or consecrated** before they are consumed. The High Priest or Priestess may say a prayer or blessing over the cakes, invoking the elements or the deities, and thanking the Earth for its abundance. The blessing may sound something like:

" "Blessed be this bread, made from the grains of the Earth, in gratitude for the sustenance it provides. May it nourish our bodies and our spirits."

M **Ale (or Wine)**: Ale or wine is often used as the drink of choice in the ritual. Ale symbolizes the **masculine principle** (as mentioned earlier), while wine can represent the feminine or the Moon, depending on the traditions of the group. In some Wiccan circles, the drink may also be a symbolic offering to the deities, especially the Horned God (associated with wine and other fermented beverages). The drink, like the cakes, is often **blessed** or **consecrated** during the ritual, and the Priest or Priestess may say something like:

" "Blessed be this drink, made from the fruits of the Earth. May it renew our spirits and connect us with the flow of the universe. [21]"

b. Sharing the Cakes and Ale

M **The High Priest and Priestess**: The ritual often involves the **High Priest and Priestess** being the first to partake of the cakes and ale, as they represent the deities and are the spiritual leaders of the group. After blessing the cakes and ale, they may share a symbolic first bite or sip. The sharing of food and drink between the Priest and Priestess can also represent the sacred marriage or divine union between the God and Goddess.

M **The Group Participants**: After the High Priest and Priestess have partaken, the cakes and ale are passed around the circle to the other members. In some traditions, the cakes and ale are passed clockwise around the circle, symbolizing the flow of energy and unity. Everyone partakes of the cakes and ale, often in silence or with a brief blessing or prayer, expressing gratitude for the experience and the divine presence.

c. The Blessing and Affirmation

Once the cakes and ale have been shared, the group may pause to reflect on the ritual, its purpose, and its outcomes. Often, participants will take a moment to give thanks for the food and drink, for the Earth's abundance, and for the divine forces that have helped in the ritual's work. This moment can be a silent one or may involve a communal chant, such as:

M "Blessed be this cake and this ale, and the spirit of love that binds us here."

The Deeper Spiritual Significance

The Cakes and Ale ceremony, while simple in practice, carries profound spiritual significance. Here are a few deeper meanings that can be found in this part of the ritual:

M **A Communion with the Divine**: The sharing of cakes and ale symbolizes the concept of **communion**—not only a physical sharing of food and drink but also a spiritual communion with the divine, the Earth, and the elements. This sharing is a sacred act, acknowledging the interconnectedness of all things.

M **Honoring the Cycle of Life**: By consuming the cakes and ale, Wiccans metaphorically partake in the cycle of life, acknowledging the Earth's cycles of birth, growth, decay, and renewal. In many ways, the act of eating and drinking becomes a spiritual affirmation of life's eternal nature.

M **Gratitude and Celebration**: The Cakes and Ale ceremony is often seen as an opportunity to express gratitude to the gods and the Earth. It's a way of celebrating life's blessings and recognizing that the Earth provides not just physically but spiritually. It helps to ground the group and prepare for closing the ritual with a sense of completion and peace.

M **Personal Empowerment**: After a ritual in which energy has been raised, the food and drink help to "ground" the participants, bringing them back to the physical world. It can be a reminder that magic is not just an abstract concept but something that works in the material world—food sustains the body, just as magic sustains the spirit.

Variations in the Ritual

The specifics of the Cakes and Ale ceremony may vary depending on the tradition of the group, its size, and the preferences of the participants. Some congregations might use wine, while others may choose fruit juices or other drinks to reflect their personal practices or to accommodate dietary restrictions. Similarly, the cakes may differ in ingredients based on personal or regional preferences. In some cases, cakes may be replaced by other food items such as honey or fruit.[22]

13, 14, and 15. Grounding and closing out the ritual.

Grounding Remaining Energy

Grounding is a way of releasing any excess energy that was raised during the ritual. This helps bring balance and ensures that no energy is left unresolved. There are several methods to ground energy:

Methods of Grounding:

M **Visualizing the Energy Returning to the Earth**:

" Stand with your feet planted firmly on the ground or sit in a meditative posture. Close your eyes and visualize the energy you raised flowing from your body and into the Earth, like roots of a tree anchoring you. Feel it sink deep into the soil, neutralizing any excess energy and returning it to nature.

" You can also imagine a cord or beam of light from your body connecting you to the Earth, with energy flowing back down into the Earth's core, balancing you and the ritual space.

M **Breathing to Release Energy**:

" Inhale deeply, hold for a few seconds, then exhale slowly while imagining that all excess energy is being released from your body with each breath. Do this until you feel settled and calm.

M **Using Physical Objects (Optional)**:

" **Crystals**: Hold a grounding crystal (like black tourmaline or hematite) in your hand. As you focus on the crystal, envision it absorbing the excess energy and anchoring you to the Earth.

" **Earth**: If you're outside, you can literally touch the earth, soil, or rocks with your hands or feet, allowing the Earth to absorb the energy.

Saying Farewell to the Quarters (Elements)

At this stage, you respectfully thank and dismiss the elemental forces (Earth, Air, Fire, Water) and any deities or spirits that you invoked. This helps to close the energy of the elements and any spiritual connections.

Process:

M **Thanking the Quarters**:

" You typically begin in the East (Air) and move around the circle in a counter-clockwise (widdershins) direction, thanking each element in turn.

" For example, you might say something like:

East (Air): "We thank the element of Air for your presence and assistance in this circle. We release you with love and gratitude. Hail and farewell."

South (Fire): "We thank the element of Fire for your energy and warmth. We release you with love and gratitude. Hail and farewell."

West (Water): "We thank the element of Water for your flow and intuition. We release you with love and gratitude. Hail and farewell."

North (Earth): "We thank the element of Earth for your stability and strength. We release you with love and gratitude. Hail and farewell."

WHY WICCA

" You may also address any specific deities, spirits, or ancestors you invoked, saying:

"We thank [name of deity/spirit] for your guidance and presence. We now bid you farewell with love and respect. Blessed be."

M **Releasing Energy**:

" After thanking each element, make sure to **visualize the energy** of that element flowing back to its place of origin. You may see the colors or symbols associated with each element dissipating or returning to nature.

Closing the Circle

Once the quarters are dismissed, the circle is formally closed. In Wicca, the circle is considered sacred space, and it needs to be "opened" and "closed" with intention. This is usually done by the High Priestess or Priest.

Steps for Closing the Circle:

M **Reversing the Opening Process**:

" If the circle was cast deosil (clockwise) at the beginning of the ritual, you will now close it widdershins (counter-clockwise). This is symbolic of returning the energy to its source and ending the sacred space.

M **Physically or Symbolically Closing the Circle**:

" If you used a wand, athame (ritual knife), or another tool to cast the circle, you will now use it to close the circle, either by retracing the circle's boundary in the reverse direction or by drawing an X or closing motion in the air. Some practitioners also touch the ground at the point where they began the circle to signify the completion.

M **Spoken Words for Closing**:

" The High Priest or Priestess may say:

\# "The circle is now closed, but never broken. As we leave this sacred space, may we carry the blessings of the ritual with us. So mote it be."

" Some rituals include an additional closing prayer or chant that acknowledges the end of the sacred work and asks for protection as the energy is released.

16. Clean up the Altar (especially important if this is not a permanent ritual space, in a group setting the duties are shared among the participants):

Remove Offerings

> *M* Food and Drink: If you've placed offerings on your altar, such as cakes, ale, incense, or herbs, you will need to properly dispose of them. Offerings are a way of showing respect, so it's important to handle them with care.
>
> " **Food offerings**: Leftover cakes or fruit can be left outside in a natural space, like your garden or a forest, as a gesture of giving back to the Earth. Some prefer to bury them, while others may scatter them[23].
>
> " **Drink offerings**: Any wine or ale can be poured out onto the ground, particularly at a place where it can return to nature. Pouring it onto the Earth or in a garden is a respectful way of releasing it back into the environment.[24]
>
> " **Flowers and other natural offerings**: If you used flowers, leaves, or herbs, you can return them to the Earth by laying them outside, composting them, or respectfully placing them in a place where they can decompose naturally.

Cleanse the Tools

Cleansing your altar tools after use is important for maintaining their energetic purity and effectiveness. The goal is to release any accumulated energy and prepare them for future use. Here's how you can cleanse different items on your altar:

M **Athame (Ritual Knife)**: If you've used the athame in the ritual, it's a good idea to cleanse it by passing it through the smoke of incense (like sage or palo santo), or by holding it over a flame briefly (but safely). Some people also pass it through a bowl of salt or water to purify it.

M **Wand**: If you used a wand, cleanse it by passing it through incense smoke or simply by wiping it with a cloth. You may also choose to bury it in the Earth for a short time or place it under moonlight to "recharge" and cleanse.

M **Chalice**: After using the chalice in a ritual, you can cleanse it by washing it gently with water. If it's been used for a special offering (like wine or ale), cleanse it with incense or by passing it through the smoke.

M **Candles and Candleholders**: If you used candles on your altar, ensure they are fully extinguished. If the candles are made of wax and have been burned down significantly, clean the holders with a soft cloth or a damp paper towel. You can also use saltwater to cleanse the holders.

M **Crystals**: Crystals are powerful tools in Wicca and can absorb energy, so it's important to cleanse them regularly. You can cleanse them by:

" Running them under cold water (if the crystal is water-safe).

" Using incense smoke (such as sage or lavender).

" Leaving them in the moonlight overnight (especially during a full moon) to recharge.

" Placing them on a selenite plate or using other cleansing stones like clear quartz.

M **Incense holders**: Clean your incense holder after use to remove any residue or ash. You can do this with a soft cloth or by gently wiping with water. Let it dry fully before placing it back on your altar.

Take Down Ritual Decorations

If you used any special symbols, sigils, or decorations for a particular ritual (e.g., pentagrams, god/goddess images, etc.), you should respectfully remove them and store them in a safe place. If you used seasonal decorations for a Sabbat, it's a good idea to put them away according to the appropriate time of year.

5. Clean and Reorganize the Altar

Once the ritual tools are cleansed and offerings have been disposed of, it's time to clean and reorganize the altar. This helps maintain a fresh and energetically balanced space.

M **Wipe Down the Altar Surface**: Use a soft cloth, and if you like, you can use a mild, natural cleaner or a solution of water and salt to wipe the surface. If you use salt, make sure it doesn't leave any residue.

M **Rearrange Tools and Symbols**: After cleaning the altar, rearrange your tools and symbols[25]. This is a good time to check if anything needs to be replaced or if any items need to be recharged (e.g., crystals, candles). Some practitioners like to refresh their altar with new flowers, fresh herbs, or other seasonal items, if it is a permanent altar.

Put Away Tools and Items

After you've cleaned everything, it's time to store your ritual tools properly. Some tips for storing:

- **Sacred Tools**: Store your tools like the athame, wand, chalice, and pentacle in a special box or pouch to protect them from dust or accidental damage. Ensure they are placed in a safe, respectful place when not in use, away from areas of mundane activity.

- **Incense and Candles**: Keep incense sticks or cones in an airtight container to keep them dry and fresh. Store candles in a cool, dry place to prevent them from melting or becoming misshapen.

- **Crystals**: Store crystals in a special box or pouch to prevent them from being damaged or scratched. Some people use cloth pouches, velvet boxes, or wooden chests to keep them safe.

- **Books and Sacred Writings**: If you've used a Book of Shadows or any other sacred texts, ensure they are kept in a safe and respectful place, away from direct sunlight or places where they may be damaged.

- **Cleansing Tools**: If you used salt, water, or other elements for cleansing, ensure they are put away properly. For example, salt can be stored in a small jar, and water in a dish.

Final Blessing and Gratitude

Once everything is cleaned and stored, you might want to take a moment to offer a final prayer of gratitude for the ritual. This can be a simple thank you to the divine, the Earth, or any spiritual beings you invoked during the ceremony. It's a gesture of respect for the energies involved. Not all groups and certainly not all solitaries do this, but it is a good idea.

Example:

M "Thank you for the guidance and energy shared during this ritual. May our work be protected and carried forward. Blessed be."

Chapter Ten - New Aeon Generic Ritual Outline –

Stage	Actions
Meet and Greet	Participants socialize before ritual
Introduction and Preparation	Participant introductions. Purpose of ritual and workings explained. Cover interesting details or facts about the nature of the event. Prepare needed materials.
Cast Circle	HP/S cast circle with athame, wand, or staff. May be done by one or the other, individually, or jointly. Circle of power cast thrice about Keep our energies in and all others out Outside of space and time this night Now in the Temple of Astral Light
Call Quarters	Hail to the Guardians of the _____ Rulers of the Element of _____ Come Now and lend your power to our rites and guard our Circle. Hail and Welcome!

Set Wards (optional)	Flamekeepers (when present)[26]
	Lady of a thousand faces, mother of us all
	Nurture us and grant us peace in all things great and small
	Bless us now and bathe us in your gentle healing glow
	Come to us and be with us that your love we may know
	Blessed Be She!
Invoke Deity	Lord of Nature, Guardian, Father of All Things
	Empower us and give us courage to handle what life brings
	Grant us all now inner strength and fill us with your power
	Join us here and join us now in this place and in this hour
	Blessed Be He!
HP/S Introduction	HP/S greet participants and reaffirm statement of purpose and intent. Any last minute questions are answered.

Meditation	Participants meditate or participate in guided meditation to help facilitate full involvement in the ritual.
Ritual Working	Conduct ritual workings (create objects, prepare slips with intention, empower objects, etc.)
Energy Raising	Raise energy through dance, chants, etc.
Energy Release	When energy reaches a crescendo, HP/S release energy toward desired objective.
Grounding	Participants are guided to ground, center, and release excess energy.
Cakes and Ale	HP/S Bless cakes and ale and distribute to participants: I Bless this food that it may nourish and sustain us I Bless this drink that it hydrate us and quench our thirst
HP/S Closing	HP/S makes closing comments, statements and observations. Participants ask questions and share their thoughts and experiences

Thank Deity	Oh Mother Goddess, Lady of Light

Accept our thanks and humble adorations

Be with us now and always

Blessed Be She

Oh Father God, Protector of us all

We offer our thanks and will honor you always

Be ever in our hearts and ever on our minds

Blessed Be He |
| Dismiss Quarters | Hail to the Guardians of the _____

Rulers of the Element of _____

Thank you for granting us your assistance and protection

Go now in peace, until we call upon you again

Hail and Farewell! |
| Take Down Circle | HP/S take down circle. Excess energy is released into the earth or an object. |

Libations	One or more participants take libations outside and make an offering.[27] Social gathering to follow.

A Note from the Paramount Priest of the Church of the New Aeon:

The New Aeon Tradition: Omnism in Wicca

The New Aeon Wiccan Tradition stands out within the broader Wiccan landscape due to its unique omnistic focus, blending the mystical, nature-centered practices of Wicca with the universal inclusivity of Omnism. This tradition embraces the belief that all spiritual paths hold pieces of the greater truth, encouraging practitioners to seek wisdom from a diverse array of religious and philosophical systems. At its core, the New Aeon Tradition reflects a harmonious synthesis of spiritual pluralism and traditional Wiccan frameworks.

Central Tenets of New Aeon Omnistic Wicca

Omnistic Wicca operates on the understanding that no single path possesses absolute authority or the entirety of divine knowledge. Practitioners recognize the beauty and sacredness in the rites and beliefs of other faiths, incorporating elements from various spiritual traditions into their rituals, meditations, and magical workings. This approach deepens personal growth and spiritual connection by weaving together threads of commonality found across cultures and belief systems.

While traditional Wiccan covens might strictly adhere to rituals passed down through lineage or specific teachings, New Aeon Wiccans view spiritual exploration as an evolving, personal journey. Each practitioner is encouraged to study multiple traditions—whether that be Buddhism, Hinduism, indigenous practices, Kabbalah, or Druidry—and to shape their practice in alignment with their personal experiences, cultural background, and inner guidance. This freedom to craft individualized spiritual paths sets New Aeon Wicca apart as an adaptive and inclusive tradition.

Ritual Structure and Practice

Despite this eclectic approach, the New Aeon Tradition retains the foundational ritual framework of Wicca. Rituals often follow the standard Wiccan format of casting a circle, calling the quarters, invoking the divine, and celebrating the cycles of the moon and sabbats. However, the deities invoked, tools used, and symbols employed may differ widely from one practitioner to another, reflecting the omnistic values of the tradition.

For instance, a New Aeon Wiccan might invoke deities from different pantheons within the same ritual or blend Eastern meditation techniques with Western ceremonial magic. A Beltane celebration could honor both the Celtic fire god Bel and the Hindu goddess Lakshmi, symbolizing a fusion of abundance and renewal drawn from multiple spiritual currents. Such rituals honor the sacred unity underlying all faiths while emphasizing Wicca's reverence for nature and the cycles of life.

The Role of Ethical Responsibility

The guiding principle of the Wiccan Rede, "An it harm none, do what ye will," remains central to New Aeon Wicca, but is expanded through the lens of omnism to emphasize global compassion and interconnectedness. Practitioners are encouraged to consider the broader implications of their actions, fostering a sense of shared responsibility for the well-being of the planet and all its inhabitants.

Inclusivity and Personal Development

One of the most distinctive features of New Aeon Wicca is its unwavering commitment to spiritual inclusivity. Covens and solitary practitioners alike create sacred spaces that welcome people of all faiths, backgrounds, and identities. This inclusivity extends to ritual design, where participants are encouraged to contribute elements from their own spiritual heritages, fostering an environment of mutual respect and shared learning.

The tradition also emphasizes personal sovereignty and empowerment. Rather than adhering to dogma, practitioners are urged to trust their intuition and inner voice. This path nurtures spiritual autonomy, allowing individuals to cultivate a practice that feels authentic and deeply resonant with their unique worldview.

A Tradition for the New Age

In an era characterized by globalization and increasing spiritual interconnectedness, the New Aeon Tradition reflects the evolving nature of contemporary spirituality. By drawing from the wellsprings of many traditions while anchoring itself in Wiccan ritual, it offers a dynamic and adaptable path that speaks to modern seekers. In celebrating the diversity of spiritual expression, New Aeon Omnistic Wicca fosters unity, compassion, and reverence for the sacred mysteries that bind all of humanity.

Ultimately, the New Aeon Tradition serves as a bridge between the familiar structure of Wicca and the expansive possibilities of omnistic practice. It is a vibrant testament to the belief that the divine reveals itself in countless ways and that by honoring this multiplicity, practitioners can cultivate a richer, more profound spiritual life.

Chapter Eleven – Sample Rituals from Various Traditions

All religions in one way or another create sacred space as we have discussed prior. Churches and Synagogues are sanctified and blessed. Priests at the beginning of Mass process around the altar, or in some liturgical traditions around the sanctuary, with incense and holy water, preceded by a crucifer and accompanied by acolytes with lit candles. This procession is intended, or was originally, to create sacred space, to protect worshipers from negative energies or beings and also to open a "portal" to the divine realms so that divine energy can infuse the worshipers.

I was stunned at the similarities to the opening of Wiccan and neoPagan ceremonies when I first attended Tim Lake's group in Schenectady, NY. I could pick out all of the elements, even though they were presented a bit differently, and came from older spiritual traditions, containing methods that are forgotten in the Abrahamic religions, except for some mystery schools that still exist within the various Abrahamic faiths.

I am going to start by listing the elements and directions as a refresher, and then outline a generic ritual of worship based on the regular ritual at the Schenectady Pagan Cluster, at Trinity Temple and at Spiral Path Temple which was very similar to one another and also to some other groups of which I am aware. This is a group ritual, with the groups that I've attended sometimes having upwards of a hundred or more participants in a given ritual.

In Wicca, the elemental forces are recognized, and saluted in the cardinal directions, each having a direction in which they are the dominant energy.
North Earth Winter
West Water Fall
South Fire Summer
East Air Spring

The fifth elemental force, Spirit, is considered centered in the individual and therefore is not assigned a direction. If I were to assign it one, that direction would be upwards, above and connecting all the others with the worshipers.

So starting the ritual, the priest and priestess, or the ritualist if there is only one, will generally call the people into a calm, meditative state, and then, either alone or with help from congregants, begin calling the directions, starting with the direction of the season that is occurring where the ceremony is being held, and working clockwise through the directions. (Please note that there will be a number of different rituals given later in this section for different Wiccan paths of worship - but here I am giving a very generic sample of what I've experienced, for explicative purposes.)

Generic Ritual based on some groups in the Northeast US

Simple Ritual (based on the Schenectady Pagan Cluster Rituals and also on rituals at Trinity Temple and Spiral Path Temple):

Salutations (starting here in Summer for purposes of this example):

(At the Southern station) "Hail Guardians of the Watchtowers of the South, Lords of Fire. Bright ones guide and light our path with fiery might and grace. We honor you with hearts alight, as the summer sun does shine. May your strength infuse our rites and your power our circle bind." (Candle is lit)

(At the Western station) "Hail Guardians of the Watchtowers of the West, Lords of Water. Masters of the flowing sea, cleanse us we ask. We invite your gentle embrace. May your wisdom and your peace guide us through our sacred rites. Join us in this sacred rite, and bind our circle tight." (Candle is lit)

(At the Northern station) "Hail Guardians of the Watchtowers of the North, Lords of Earth. Masters of death and rebirth. Guardians of the ancient land. We honor you with reverence for your strength and grace, and for your guiding hand in death and rebirth. As the seasons turn anew, join us as we journey through dark and light, and make our circle strong tonight." (Candle is lit)

(At the Eastern Station) "Hail Guardians of the Watchtowers of the East, Lords of Air. Keepers of the winds and skies. We honor you and your airy realm with your whispers of wisdom bringing clarity to our minds. We honor you protectors of the dawn and welcome your power to our circle tonight (Candle is lit).

Now, the priestess, or the priestess and the priest (or the ritualist) with athame (sacred knife) or wand circles the altar, or the entire congregation three times. Generally that circling is done clockwise, although in some circumstances and traditions it may be counter clockwise.

The first circle is made with the athame or wand pointed to the floor, the second circle is made with the athame or wand at waist height. The third time with the athame or wand pointing upwards

(At the main altar, Priest and Priestess or Priest OR Priestess):

Priestess: "Great Goddess, Mother of all things, Queen of the moon and stars. We honor you and welcome you to our circle. Bless this sacred space with your divine feminine energy, and guide us in our sacred rites." (candle is lit)

Priest: "Great God, Father of all things, King of the sun and forest. We honor you and welcome you to our circle. Bless this sacred space with your divine masculine energy, and protect us in our sacred rites." (candle is lit)

Note: Some groups or individual practitioners may also invoke the spirits of the ancestors or the fey at this point (a fully fey ritual will be included in the Variant ritual chapter.) if you invoke one or both of those groups - here are some suggested words:

To invoke the fey: "Spirits of the Fey, guardians of the wild places, creatures of magic and moonlight. We welcome you to our circle. Join us in our revels, share your joy and wisdom. Dance with us beneath the stars, and bless this circle with your enchantment." (candle may be lit - some ritualists leave out a candle for the fey, viewing the invitation itself as enough)

To invoke the ancestors: "Beloved Ancestors, spirits of our blood and bone, keepers of our ancient wisdom. We honor you and call upon your presence. Join us in this sacred circle, guide and protect us. Share your love and wisdom, and bless our rites with your ancestral strength." (candle is lit)

Since this is a congregate setting, now that sacred space has been established, the watchtowers set, and those supernal beings who are wanted to join the ritual invited, there may be conversation, discussion, announcements, and even a short sermon (every group I've attended had a short sermon, never more than 5 minutes or so, and usually related to the holiday.).

Then there will be the equivalent of prayer or spellwork led by the priestess and priest or by the ritualist. Often appropriate to the holiday, and often, even in urban settings, very much related to farming and rural life. Planting, good farming weather, harvest, the turn of the year, and so forth dominate the broader ritual relevance, along with invoking healing for the sick, strength for the weak, and justice for the downtrodden.

This section of the worship may include gathering of energy, often through singing, dancing, drumming and other related things while the participants focus on the goal of the work. When that is finished one of two things will happen.

The Great Feast. This looks like Eucharist and may be one of the precursors to Eucharist. Cakes and ale, or bread and juice, or something and wine – another words, one food and one drink item. These are distributed to the congregates and then the following type of invocations occur:

Priest (holding up the food item): "By the bounty of the Lord, may you never hunger" (everyone repeats and reverently eats the food item).

Priestess (holding up the drink item): "By the bounty of the Lady, may you never thirst.[28]"

Together, or another preselected congregate: "With the spirits of the ancestors may you never be alone."

Alterations to the generic ritual given for the Sabbats –

1. Samhain (October 31 - November 1)

Theme: End of the harvest, honoring ancestors, the thinning of the veil between worlds.

Ritual:

- **Preparation:** Set up an altar with photos of ancestors, seasonal decorations (pumpkins, autumn leaves), and offerings (food, drinks).

- **Circle Casting:** Cast a circle to create sacred space.

- **Invocation:** Call upon deities associated with the dead, such as Hecate or the God of the Underworld.

- **Meditation:** Spend time in meditation or silent reflection to connect with ancestors.

- **Offering:** Light candles or incense and offer food/drink to ancestors, symbolizing the honoring of their spirits.

- **Divination:** Perform a divination practice (tarot, runes) to seek guidance for the coming year.

- **Feasting:** Share a meal with loved ones, incorporating seasonal foods.

2. Yule (Winter Solstice, around December 21)

Theme: Celebration of the rebirth of the Sun, hope, and renewal.

Ritual:

- **Preparation:** Decorate the altar with evergreen branches, a Yule log, and candles (representing the Sun).

- **Circle Casting:** Cast a circle, focusing on warmth and light.

- **Invocation:** Call upon solar deities like the God or the Great Mother.

- **Lighting the Yule Log:** Light the Yule log, symbolizing the return of light.

- **Gift Exchange:** Share small gifts to celebrate generosity and love.

- **Intentions:** Write down intentions or wishes for the coming year and burn them in the flame of the Yule log.

- **Feasting:** Enjoy a feast featuring seasonal foods like roasted meats, nuts, and spiced beverage

3. Imbolc (February 1-2)

- s. **Theme:** Awakening of the earth, purification, and the return of light.

Ritual:

- Preparation: Create an altar with candles, white flowers, and symbols of Brigid (like a Brigid's cross).

- **Circle Casting:** Cast a circle focusing on purification and new beginnings.

- **Invocation:** Call upon Brigid or other deities of light and inspiration.

- **Candle Ritual:** Light candles, symbolizing the returning light and the spark of creativity.

- **Purification:** Use water or salt to cleanse objects or spaces, representing renewal.

М **Crafting:** Engage in a creative activity (e.g., writing, crafting) to honor inspiration.

М **Feasting:** Share foods that represent the season, such as dairy products, bread, and seeds.

4. Ostara (Spring Equinox, around March 21)

Theme: Fertility, balance, and new growth.

Ritual:

М Preparation: Set up an altar with eggs, flowers, and seeds.

М **Circle Casting:** Cast a circle, focusing on balance and growth.

М **Invocation:** Call upon fertility deities like Ostara or Persephone.

М **Egg Decorating:** Decorate eggs as symbols of new life and potential.

М **Seed Planting:** Plant seeds in the ground or pots, symbolizing future growth.

М **Balancing Exercise:** Perform a balance exercise (yoga, walking on a line) to symbolize the equinox.

М **Feasting:** Enjoy a meal featuring fresh greens and spring vegetables.

5. Beltane (May 1)

Theme: Fertility, passion, and the celebration of life.

Ritual:

М Preparation: Decorate the altar with flowers, greenery, and symbols of fertility.

- **Circle Casting:** Cast a circle, inviting the energy of passion and creativity.

- **Invocation:** Call upon the Great Horned God and the Goddess of fertility.

- **Maypole Dance:** If possible, perform a maypole dance to symbolize the union of male and female energies.

- **Fire Ritual:** Light a bonfire or candles to represent passion and purification.

- **Flower Offering:** Create flower crowns or offerings to honor the Earth and beauty.

- **Feasting:** Share a feast of fruits, flowers, and seasonal delights.

6. Litha (Summer Solstice, around June 21)

Theme: The height of summer, abundance, and celebration of the Sun.

Ritual:

- Preparation: Set up an altar with sun symbols, flowers, and herbs.

- **Circle Casting:** Cast a circle, inviting the energy of abundance and joy.

- **Invocation:** Call upon solar deities like the Sun God or Goddesses of harvest.

- **Sun Appreciation:** Spend time outdoors, honoring the sun's energy through meditation or rituals.

- **Herb Gathering:** Gather herbs associated with the season for future use in spells or potions.

- **M Fire Ritual:** Light a bonfire or candles, celebrating the power of the Sun.

- **M Feasting:** Enjoy a summer feast featuring fresh fruits, vegetables, and grilled foods.

7. *Lammas (Lughnasadh, August 1)*

Theme: The first harvest, gratitude, and abundance.

Ritual:

- M Preparation: Set up an altar with grains, bread, and seasonal fruits.

- **M Circle Casting:** Cast a circle focusing on gratitude and abundance.

- **M Invocation:** Call upon the Grain God and the Goddess of harvest.

- **M Bread Baking:** Bake bread or prepare a grain-based dish as an offering.

- **M Gratitude Sharing:** Share what you are grateful for from the past year.

- **M Harvest Ritual:** Gather fruits or grains, symbolizing the abundance of the land.

- **M Feasting:** Celebrate with a harvest feast, incorporating bread and seasonal produce.

8. *Mabon (Autumn Equinox, around September 21)*

Theme: Reflection, balance, and the second harvest.

Ritual:

> M Preparation: Set up an altar with autumn leaves, fruits, and seasonal decorations.
>
> M **Circle Casting:** Cast a circle focusing on reflection and balance.
>
> M **Invocation:** Call upon deities of harvest and change.
>
> M **Balance Meditation:** Meditate on personal balance and what to release as the season changes.
>
> M **Gratitude Offering:** Create an offering of fruits or grains for the Earth.
>
> M **Reflection:** Write down lessons learned during the year and what you wish to release.
>
> M **Feasting:** Share a meal featuring harvest foods like apples, pumpkins, and root vegetables.

Variant Rituals (Dragon Based Ritual)

1. Samhain (October 31 - November 1)

Theme: Honoring ancestors and connecting with the spirit world.

Ritual:

> M Preparation: Create a sacred space with images of dragons representing protection and transformation. Set up an ancestor altar with offerings (food, flowers).
>
> M **Opening Circle:** Gather participants in a circle and light a central candle, invoking the presence of the Dragon Spirits.
>
> M **Invocation:** Call upon the Dragon of Shadows to guide you through the veil. Participants can share names or stories of ancestors.

M **Connection with Ancestors:** Each participant lights a candle in honor of their ancestors, visualizing a protective dragon guiding their spirits.

M **Dragon Divination:** Use a dragon oracle deck or crystals to seek guidance from dragon energies for the coming year.

M **Feasting:** Share seasonal foods and offerings with the dragon spirits and ancestors.

2. *Yule (Winter Solstice, around December 21)*

Theme: Rebirth of the Sun and renewal.

Ritual:

M Preparation: Decorate an altar with winter-themed dragon imagery, evergreen branches, and a Yule log.

M **Opening Circle:** Gather around the Yule log, lighting a candle for each participant.

M **Invocation:** Call upon the Fire Dragon for warmth and renewal. Share intentions for the new year.

M **Yule Log Ceremony:** Each participant writes an intention on a piece of paper and attaches it to the Yule log before lighting it, symbolizing the return of the Sun.

M **Dragon Dance:** Encourage participants to express joy through movement, channeling the energy of the Fire Dragon.

M **Feasting:** Enjoy a festive meal, leaving an offering of food for the dragons and the spirit of Yule.

3. Imbolc (February 1-2)

Theme: Awakening, inspiration, and purification.

Ritual:

> M Preparation: Create an altar with white candles, crystals, and dragon images representing purity and creativity.
>
> M **Opening Circle:** Gather in a circle and light a central candle.
>
> M **Invocation:** Call upon the Dragon of Light (or a specific dragon associated with Brigid) to inspire creativity.
>
> M **Candle Lighting Ceremony:** Each participant lights a candle from the central flame, visualizing the spark of creativity igniting within them.
>
> M **Creative Expression:** Invite participants to create art, poetry, or music inspired by the Dragon of Light.
>
> M **Feasting:** Share a meal of dairy and bread, dedicating the meal to the dragons and the energy of inspiration.

4. Ostara (Spring Equinox, around March 21)

Theme: Fertility, balance, and new growth.

Ritual:

> M Preparation: Set up an altar with spring flowers, eggs, and dragon imagery representing fertility.
>
> M **Opening Circle:** Gather in a circle, planting seeds in small pots, each symbolizing a hope or intention for growth.

M **Invocation:** Call upon the Earth Dragon to bless the seeds and intentions shared.

M **Egg Decorating:** Provide eggs for participants to decorate with symbols of their intentions. Create a communal altar with these eggs.

M **Balance Meditation:** Lead a guided meditation connecting with the Earth Dragon, focusing on balance and new beginnings.

M **Feasting:** Enjoy a meal featuring fresh greens and seasonal foods, sharing offerings with the Earth Dragon.

5. Beltane (May 1)

Theme: Celebration of life, passion, and fertility.

Ritual:

M **Preparation:** Create a vibrant altar with flowers, ribbons, and dragon images representing passion and fertility.

M **Opening Circle:** Gather participants around a maypole.

M **Invocation:** Call upon the Fire Dragon and the Dragon of Love. Participants can share what they celebrate.

M **Maypole Dance:** Engage in a maypole dance, weaving ribbons together and inviting the dragons to bless the celebration.

M **Flower Offering:** Create flower crowns or offerings for the dragons, symbolizing beauty and fertility.

M **Feasting:** Celebrate with a festive meal of fruits, flowers, and sweet treats, dedicating the feast to the dragons.

6. Litha (Summer Solstice, around June 21)

Theme: Abundance, joy, and celebration of the Sun.

Ritual:

> M Preparation: Set up an altar with sun symbols, herbs, and dragon imagery representing abundance.
>
> M **Opening Circle:** Gather outside or in a bright space, lighting candles or a bonfire.
>
> M **Invocation:** Call upon the Solar Dragon and nature spirits. Participants can express what brings them joy.
>
> M **Sun Appreciation Ceremony:** Lead participants in a meditation to absorb the sun's energy, visualizing the Solar Dragon filling them with light.
>
> M **Herb Gathering:** Invite participants to share herbs associated with summer, creating a communal herbal offering for the dragons.
>
> M **Feasting:** Share a summer feast of fresh fruits and vegetables, honoring the dragons' energy.

7. Lammas (Lughnasadh, August 1)

Theme: The first harvest, gratitude, and sharing.

Ritual:

> M Preparation: Create an altar with grains, fruits, and dragon imagery representing harvest and gratitude.

- **Opening Circle:** Gather participants and light a central candle, sharing what they are thankful for.

- **Invocation:** Call upon the Harvest Dragon to bless the gathering and the foods.

- **Bread Baking Ceremony:** If possible, bake bread together or share pre-baked bread. Each participant can contribute a piece as an offering.

- **Gratitude Sharing:** Create a communal offering of the harvested foods for the dragons, dedicating it to the Earth.

- **Feasting:** Enjoy a communal meal, featuring the bread and other harvest foods, celebrating abundance.

8. Mabon (Autumn Equinox, around September 21)

Theme: Reflection, balance, and gratitude for the harvest.

Ritual:

- Preparation: Set up an altar with autumn leaves, fruits, and dragon imagery representing reflection and gratitude.

- **Opening Circle:** Gather in a circle, lighting candles to symbolize balance.

- **Invocation:** Call upon the Autumn Dragon and deities of harvest. Participants can share what they wish to release and what they are thankful for.

- **Balance Meditation:** Lead a meditation focusing on gratitude and balance, inviting the Autumn Dragon to guide participants.

- **Gratitude Offering:** Create a communal offering of fruits or grains for the dragons, expressing thanks for their guidance throughout the year.

- **Feasting:** Celebrate with a meal featuring autumnal foods, sharing offerings with the dragons.

Variant Ritual (Faery Based Ritual)

1. Samhain (October 31 - November 1)

Theme: Honoring ancestors and connecting with the spirit world.

Ritual:

- **Preparation:** Create a sacred space with images of dragons representing protection and transformation. Set up an ancestor altar with offerings (food, flowers).

- **Opening Circle:** Gather participants in a circle and light a central candle, invoking the presence of the Dragon Spirits.

- **Invocation:** Call upon the Dragon of Shadows to guide you through the veil. Participants can share names or stories of ancestors.

- **Connection with Ancestors:** Each participant lights a candle in honor of their ancestors, visualizing a protective dragon guiding their spirits.

- **Dragon Divination:** Use a dragon oracle deck or crystals to seek guidance from dragon energies for the coming year.

- **Feasting:** Share seasonal foods and offerings with the dragon spirits and ancestors.

2. Yule (Winter Solstice, around December 21)

Theme: Rebirth of the Sun and renewal.

Ritual:

M Preparation: Decorate an altar with winter-themed dragon imagery, evergreen branches, and a Yule log.

M **Opening Circle:** Gather around the Yule log, lighting a candle for each participant.

M **Invocation:** Call upon the Fire Dragon for warmth and renewal. Share intentions for the new year.

M **Yule Log Ceremony:** Each participant writes an intention on a piece of paper and attaches it to the Yule log before lighting it, symbolizing the return of the Sun.

M **Dragon Dance:** Encourage participants to express joy through movement, channeling the energy of the Fire Dragon.

M **Feasting:** Enjoy a festive meal, leaving an offering of food for the dragons and the spirit of Yule.

3. Imbolc (February 1-2)

Theme: Awakening, inspiration, and purification.

Ritual:

M Preparation: Create an altar with white candles, crystals, and dragon images representing purity and creativity.

M **Opening Circle:** Gather in a circle and light a central candle.

- **Invocation:** Call upon the Dragon of Light (or a specific dragon associated with Brigid) to inspire creativity.

- **Candle Lighting Ceremony:** Each participant lights a candle from the central flame, visualizing the spark of creativity igniting within them.

- **Creative Expression:** Invite participants to create art, poetry, or music inspired by the Dragon of Light.

- **Feasting:** Share a meal of dairy and bread, dedicating the meal to the dragons and the energy of inspiration.

4. Ostara (Spring Equinox, around March 21)

Theme: Fertility, balance, and new growth.

Ritual:

- **Preparation:** Set up an altar with spring flowers, eggs, and dragon imagery representing fertility.

- **Opening Circle:** Gather in a circle, planting seeds in small pots, each symbolizing a hope or intention for growth.

- **Invocation:** Call upon the Earth Dragon to bless the seeds and intentions shared.

- **Egg Decorating:** Provide eggs for participants to decorate with symbols of their intentions. Create a communal altar with these eggs.

- **Balance Meditation:** Lead a guided meditation connecting with the Earth Dragon, focusing on balance and new beginnings.

- M **Feasting:** Enjoy a meal featuring fresh greens and seasonal foods, sharing offerings with the Earth Dragon.

5. Beltane (May 1)

Theme: Celebration of life, passion, and fertility.

Ritual:

- M **Preparation:** Create a vibrant altar with flowers, ribbons, and dragon images representing passion and fertility.

- M **Opening Circle:** Gather participants around a maypole.

- M **Invocation:** Call upon the Fire Dragon and the Dragon of Love. Participants can share what they celebrate.

- M **Maypole Dance:** Engage in a maypole dance, weaving ribbons together and inviting the dragons to bless the celebration.

- M **Flower Offering:** Create flower crowns or offerings for the dragons, symbolizing beauty and fertility.

- M **Feasting:** Celebrate with a festive meal of fruits, flowers, and sweet treats, dedicating the feast to the dragons.

6. Litha (Summer Solstice, around June 21)

Theme: Abundance, joy, and celebration of the Sun.

Ritual:

- M **Preparation:** Set up an altar with sun symbols, herbs, and dragon imagery representing abundance.

- **Opening Circle:** Gather outside or in a bright space, lighting candles or a bonfire.

- **Invocation:** Call upon the Solar Dragon and nature spirits. Participants can express what brings them joy.

- **Sun Appreciation Ceremony:** Lead participants in a meditation to absorb the sun's energy, visualizing the Solar Dragon filling them with light.

- **Herb Gathering:** Invite participants to share herbs associated with summer, creating a communal herbal offering for the dragons.

- **Feasting:** Share a summer feast of fresh fruits and vegetables, honoring the dragons' energy.

7. Lammas (Lughnasadh, August 1)

Theme: The first harvest, gratitude, and sharing.

Ritual:

- Preparation: Create an altar with grains, fruits, and dragon imagery representing harvest and gratitude.

- **Opening Circle:** Gather participants and light a central candle, sharing what they are thankful for.

- **Invocation:** Call upon the Harvest Dragon to bless the gathering and the foods.

- **Bread Baking Ceremony:** If possible, bake bread together or share pre-baked bread. Each participant can contribute a piece as an offering.

- **Gratitude Sharing:** Create a communal offering of the harvested foods for the dragons, dedicating it to the Earth.

- **Feasting:** Enjoy a communal meal, featuring the bread and other harvest foods, celebrating abundance.

8. Mabon (Autumn Equinox, around September 21)

Theme: Reflection, balance, and gratitude for the harvest.

Ritual:

- Preparation: Set up an altar with autumn leaves, fruits, and dragon imagery representing reflection and gratitude.

- **Opening Circle:** Gather in a circle, lighting candles to symbolize balance.

- **Invocation:** Call upon the Autumn Dragon and deities of harvest. Participants can share what they wish to release and what they are thankful for.

- **Balance Meditation:** Lead a meditation focusing on gratitude and balance, inviting the Autumn Dragon to guide participants.

- **Gratitude Offering:** Create a communal offering of fruits or grains for the dragons, expressing thanks for their guidance throughout the year.

- **Feasting:** Celebrate with a meal featuring autumnal foods, sharing offerings with the dragons.

Variant Ritual (Hermetic Style Ritual)[29]

1. Samhain (October 31 - November 1)

Theme: Death, reflection, and connecting with the spirit world.

Ritual:

M Preparation: Set up an altar with black and white candles, a skull or symbol of mortality, and representations of the Four Elements.

M **Circle Casting:** Cast a circle using salt or a wand, invoking the Four Archangels.

M **Invocation of the Ancestors:** Call upon the spirits of the ancestors using the LBRP (Lesser Banishing Ritual of the Pentagram) followed by the LIRP (Lesser Invoking Ritual of the Pentagram) to invite them.

M **Meditation:** Enter a meditative state, focusing on the connections with the spirit world. Visualize the veil thinning and the ancestors appearing.

M **Offering:** Leave food and drink as offerings for the ancestors. You may choose to read poetry or sacred texts to honor them.

M **Closing:** Thank the spirits and close the circle, extinguishing the candles.

2. Yule (Winter Solstice, around December 21)

Theme: Rebirth, renewal, and the return of the light.

Ritual:

M Preparation: Decorate the altar with evergreen branches, a Yule log, and symbols of the Sun (golden candles, sun symbols).

M **Circle Casting:** Cast a circle, invoking the elemental powers and the Archangels.

M **Invocation of the Solar Deity:** Call upon the solar deities (e.g., Helios, Apollo) for guidance and inspiration. Recite relevant passages from sacred texts.

M **Candle Ceremony:** Light a candle representing the Sun and have participants share their intentions for the coming year.

M **Yule Log Ceremony:** Each participant writes their intentions on slips of paper, attaches them to the Yule log, and burns it, symbolizing the return of the light.

M **Closing:** Thank the solar deities and close the circle.

3. *Imbolc (February 1-2)*

Theme: Awakening, inspiration, and purification.

Ritual:

M **Preparation:** Set up the altar with white candles, symbols of purity, and representations of Brigid.

M **Circle Casting:** Cast a circle using the Golden Dawn techniques, invoking the elements.

M **Invocation of Brigid:** Call upon Brigid, focusing on her aspects of creativity and inspiration. Recite prayers or invocations associated with her.

M **Candle Lighting:** Light candles representing the return of light and inspiration. Each participant can light a candle and state their intention.

- **Creative Activity:** Engage in a creative exercise (writing, drawing) inspired by the energy of Imbolc.

- **Closing:** Thank Brigid and close the circle, extinguishing the candles.

4. Ostara (Spring Equinox, around March 21)

Theme: Fertility, balance, and new beginnings.

Ritual:

- **Preparation:** Decorate the altar with spring flowers, eggs, and symbols of the elements.

- **Circle Casting:** Cast a circle, inviting the energies of growth and balance.

- **Invocation of the Earth Goddess:** Call upon the Earth Mother or a fertility deity. Use appropriate prayers or invocations.

- **Balance Meditation:** Lead a guided meditation focusing on the balance of light and dark, and the fertility of the Earth.

- **Seed Planting:** Each participant can plant seeds in small pots, symbolizing their intentions for growth.

- **Closing:** Thank the Earth Goddess and close the circle.

5. Beltane (May 1)

Theme: Passion, fertility, and celebration of life.

Ritual:

- Preparation: Set up the altar with flowers, ribbons, and symbols of fertility.

- **Circle Casting:** Cast a circle using the Golden Dawn techniques, invoking the elements and the Archangels.

- **Invocation of the God and Goddess:** Call upon the May Queen and Green Man, or equivalent deities. Recite invocations that celebrate their union.

- **Maypole Dance:** Engage in a maypole dance, weaving ribbons together to symbolize unity and fertility.

- **Offering:** Create a floral offering for the deities, asking for their blessings on your intentions.

- **Closing:** Thank the deities and close the circle.

6. Litha (Summer Solstice, around June 21)

Theme: Abundance, joy, and celebration of the Sun.

Ritual:

- Preparation: Decorate the altar with sun symbols, herbs, and seasonal fruits.

- **Circle Casting:** Cast a circle, invoking the powers of the Sun and the Four Elements.

- **Invocation of the Solar Deity:** Call upon solar deities, focusing on abundance and joy. Recite appropriate invocations or prayers.

- **Solar Meditation:** Lead a meditation to absorb the Sun's energy, visualizing golden light filling the space.

- **Herb Offering:** Create a herbal offering for the solar deities, dedicating it to the energies of abundance.

- **Closing:** Thank the solar deities and close the circle.

7. Lammas (Lughnasadh, August 1)

Theme: The first harvest, gratitude, and sharing.

Ritual:

- **Preparation:** Set up the altar with grains, fruits, and symbols of abundance.

- **Circle Casting:** Cast a circle, invoking the powers of the Earth and the Four Elements.

- **Invocation of the Harvest Deity:** Call upon deities associated with harvest, such as Demeter or Ceres. Use prayers or invocations of gratitude.

- **Gratitude Sharing:** Each participant shares what they are grateful for regarding their personal harvests and achievements.

- **Bread Ceremony:** Bake or share bread as a symbol of the harvest. Each participant can take a piece as an offering.

- **Closing:** Thank the harvest deities and close the circle.

8. Mabon (Autumn Equinox, around September 21)

Theme: Reflection, balance, and gratitude for the harvest.

Ritual:

M Preparation: Set up the altar with autumn leaves, fruits, and symbols of balance.

M **Circle Casting:** Cast a circle, invoking the powers of the Earth and the Four Elements.

M **Invocation of Autumn Deities:** Call upon deities of the harvest and the changing season. Use relevant invocations or prayers.

M **Balance Meditation:** Lead a meditation focusing on gratitude and balance as the year transitions from light to dark.

M **Gratitude Offering:** Create a communal offering of fruits or grains for the deities, expressing thanks for their guidance.

M **Closing:** Thank the autumn deities and close the circle.

Variant Ritual (solitary rituals for the sole practitioner)

1. Samhain (October 31 – November 1)

M Theme: The Veil between worlds is thinnest; honoring ancestors and the dead.

M **Ritual Ideas**:

" Light a black candle to represent the ancestors.

" Set up an ancestor altar with photographs, candles, or objects of those passed.

" Conduct a ritual of remembrance, meditating on the lives of those who have passed.

" Perform a divination ritual using tarot, runes, or a pendulum to connect with spirit guides.

" Feast on foods that connect with your ancestors' traditions.

2. Yule (Winter Solstice, around December 21)

M Theme: Birth of the Sun; rebirth and renewal.

M **Ritual Ideas:**

" Light a candle for the rebirth of the Sun. Use a red, gold, or white candle for this.

" Decorate a Yule tree with natural items like pinecones, berries, and crystals.

" Perform a meditation on new beginnings and set your intentions for the coming year.

" Create a Yule log (physically or metaphorically). This could be a small ritual where you light a log, a candle, or a piece of wood representing the return of the light.

" Perform a simple ritual to honor the Divine in its form as the Sun.

3. Imbolc (February 1-2)

M Theme: Cleansing, light, and purification; the stirring of life.

M **Ritual Ideas:**

" Honor Brigid, the goddess of healing, poetry, and smithcraft. Light candles to represent the growing light.

" Purify your space with incense or a smudge of sage, lavender, or rosemary.

" Perform a cleansing ritual for yourself or your home.

" Craft a Brigid's Cross or make a small offering of milk, honey, or bread.

" Write down your goals for personal growth, focusing on creativity, healing, or transformation.

4. Ostara (Spring Equinox, around March 20)

M Theme: Balance, fertility, and new beginnings.

M **Ritual Ideas**:

" Create an altar using flowers, eggs, and other symbols of fertility and rebirth.

" Plant seeds or bulbs in your garden or on your windowsill, symbolizing your goals for growth.

" Perform a balance ritual, perhaps focusing on balancing aspects of your life (work, relationships, etc.).

" Use eggs (real or symbolic) to represent new opportunities and wishes.

" Celebrate the balance of light and dark, reflecting on the harmony in your life.

5. Beltane (April 30 – May 1)

M Theme: Fertility, passion, and union.

M **Ritual Ideas**:

" Jump the "Beltane fire" (this can be symbolic; you can leap over candles or create a fire pit if safe).

" Decorate your space with flowers, particularly those that symbolize passion and fertility (like hawthorn or roses).

" Perform a handfasting ritual, either by yourself or with a partner, symbolizing commitment to your personal goals or self.

" Focus on passion and creativity; engage in a craft or artistic endeavor.

" Make an offering of honey, milk, or other sweet foods, honoring the life-giving energies of Beltane.

6. Litha (Summer Solstice, around June 21)

M Theme: Power, strength, and abundance.

M **Ritual Ideas**:

" Celebrate the Sun at its peak with a meditation on strength, vitality, and personal power.

" Decorate your altar with solar symbols (sunflowers, yellow flowers, gold, and orange candles).

" Conduct a ritual of empowerment, where you call upon the Sun's energy to strengthen yourself and your goals.

" Perform a nature walk, gathering herbs and flowers to honor the bounty of the Earth.

" Set intentions for success and abundance, perhaps doing a candle spell or offering to the Sun.

7. Lammas (August 1)

M Theme: First harvest, gratitude, and abundance.

M **Ritual Ideas**:

" Create a bread or harvest-themed ritual. Bake bread as an offering to the Earth.

" Honor the harvest by focusing on what you've accomplished and what you are ready to reap.

" Offer thanks for abundance in your life, both material and spiritual.

" Create a corn dolly or harvest charm to symbolize your gratitude and the year's abundance.

" Perform a ritual that acknowledges the cycles of growth and harvest, reflecting on what you've grown and learned.

8. Mabon (Autumn Equinox, around September 21)

M Theme: Gratitude, balance, and reflection.

M **Ritual Ideas**:

" Create an altar with fruits, acorns, and harvest symbols to celebrate the abundance of the Earth.

" Perform a ritual of thanksgiving, acknowledging the blessings of the past year and the balance of light and dark.

" Meditate on the balance in your life, both light and shadow, and reflect on what has been fruitful.

" Prepare a meal with seasonal foods (apples, grapes, root vegetables) to honor the Earth's abundance.

" Do a simple ritual of gratitude, writing down things you are thankful for and giving thanks to the Divine.

Virtual Ritual (Chaos rituals of self empowerment)[30]

Chaos Magic is a contemporary form of magick that emphasizes results over tradition, structure, and belief systems. It is often seen as a highly experimental and practical approach to magical work. Here's a breakdown of the key concepts behind chaos magick:

Explanation of Chaos Magick

1. *Belief as a Tool:*

Chaos magicians believe that belief itself is a powerful tool in magical practice. Unlike traditional magical systems that have fixed rituals, gods, or deities, chaos magicians view belief as a flexible and interchangeable tool. The idea is that by adopting different belief systems temporarily (such as those of a particular religion, tradition, or philosophy), you can access and manipulate the magical energies associated with those systems to achieve your goals. The practitioner doesn't need to believe in the system permanently — only for the duration of the working.

> M **Key Concept**: *"Belief is a tool, not a truth."* You can use whatever belief system works for you, but the key is to be able to let go of it when it is no longer useful.

2. *Pragmatism and Results:*

Chaos magic is results-oriented. Practitioners focus on achieving concrete outcomes, such as manifesting desires, achieving personal transformation, or altering circumstances, rather than adhering to a set of established doctrines or rituals. If a magical technique works, then it's considered valid, regardless of whether it fits within a traditional system.

> M **Key Concept**: *Results over dogma.* The effectiveness of the practice is measured by whether it brings the desired outcome, not by whether it adheres to a specific tradition.

3. *Sigils:*

One of the most popular tools in chaos magic is the use of **sigils**. A sigil is a symbol created to represent a specific desire or intention. The process of creating a sigil involves:

1. Writing down a clear, concise statement of intent (e.g., "I will get a promotion at work").
2. Removing all vowels and repeating letters to condense the sentence into a unique string of consonants.
3. Using these letters to create a symbol, or "sigil," that visually represents the intention.
4. Charging the sigil (imprinting it with energy) through focused concentration, ritual, or altered states of consciousness.
5. Finally, forgetting about the sigil, allowing the desire to manifest without attachment or interference from the conscious mind.

This method of symbolic representation allows the practitioner to bypass the conscious mind and tap into the unconscious or "magical" mind, which is believed to work more powerfully to manifest the desire.

4. Rituals and Techniques:

In chaos magic, rituals can be highly individualized and non-traditional. A practitioner might create their own rituals, modify existing ones, or borrow techniques from various magical traditions, spiritual practices, or even pop culture. The point is to work with whatever feels effective.

Some common techniques include:

> M **Meditation and Visualization**: To focus the mind on a desired outcome.

> M **Altered States of Consciousness (ASCs)**: Using techniques like breath control, sensory deprivation, drumming, or even substances (in a controlled manner) to enter a trance and increase the effectiveness of the magic.

> M **Psychodrama**: Acting out scenarios or invoking archetypes to trigger certain psychological processes that lead to the desired outcome.

> M **Reality Hacking**: This refers to methods of manipulating or changing perceptions of reality, such as using affirmations or reframing personal beliefs.

5. The Role of the Practitioner:

In chaos magick, the practitioner is seen as the central force in the working. There is no need to rely on a god or deity, though practitioners may choose to work with entities if it aligns with their goals. In fact, many chaos magicians adopt a fluid approach to spirituality, recognizing that they can work with various gods, spirits, or archetypes when they feel the need, but they don't commit to any one set of beliefs. This flexibility is one of the core tenets of chaos magic.

6. *Practicality and Innovation:*

Chaos magicians are often interested in experimental approaches to magick. They may adapt or create new techniques based on their own experiences, findings, or personal insights. This often leads to a creative, innovative approach to magic where no path is too rigid. For instance, a chaos magician might use pop culture symbols or even science fiction references to create sigils or rituals.

> M For example, a practitioner might use a symbol from a favorite book or movie (say, the symbol of a superhero or a fictional deity) as a part of their ritual or sigil work. This isn't about "believing" in those symbols in the traditional sense, but using them as a cultural trigger to influence the subconscious mind.

7. The "Prime Directive" of Chaos Magic:

Some chaos magicians use the idea of a "prime directive," which states that the ultimate goal of any magical work is to bring about personal power, self-awareness, and freedom. This means the focus is not only on the external world (manifesting desires) but also on inner transformation. Self-mastery and psychological growth are core pursuits.

8. Influences:

Chaos magic is influenced by a range of traditions and disciplines:

- **Western Occultism**: Elements from ceremonial magic, such as ritual tools and symbolism.

- **Thelema**: The philosophy and practices of Aleister Crowley.

- **Shamanism**: Use of altered states and rituals for direct interaction with the unconscious mind.

- **Psychology**: Incorporates ideas from Carl Jung (such as archetypes and the collective unconscious) and modern psychological techniques.

- **Pop Culture**: Drawing from modern myths, movies, and media, chaos magicians often incorporate symbols and ideas from contemporary culture into their practices.

Conclusion:

Chaos magick is a highly flexible and results-driven approach to magick that encourages the practitioner to be creative, experimental, and pragmatic. The use of belief as a tool, the focus on personal empowerment, and the creation of custom rituals are all central elements of chaos magick. It's a practice that thrives on adaptability and the idea that there is no one "right" way to work magic — only what works for you.

Sample outline:

1. Ritual of Personal Empowerment

Purpose: To boost confidence and personal power.

Materials:

- A small mirror

- A black candle (for banishing negativity)
- A white candle (for clarity and positivity)
- A personal symbol (e.g., a sigil)

Ritual:

1. Preparation: Find a quiet space and arrange the candles on your altar. Place the mirror in front of you.
2. **Circle Casting:** Cast a circle using your preferred method (salt, visualization, etc.).
3. **Invocation:** Call upon deities or energies that embody strength and confidence, like Athena or the warrior aspect of the God.
4. **Mirror Meditation:** Light the black candle and focus on the mirror, visualizing any negative beliefs or self-doubt being reflected back. Say, "I release what no longer serves me."
5. **Empowerment Affirmation:** Light the white candle and gaze into the mirror. Repeat affirmations such as "I am powerful. I am capable. I am worthy."
6. **Sigil Creation:** Create a sigil that represents your empowerment. Charge it with energy by visualizing its success while focusing on the candles.
7. **Closing:** Thank the energies or deities you invoked, extinguish the candles, and release the circle.

2. *Ritual of Intent and Will*

Purpose: To manifest a specific desire or goal.

Materials:

- A piece of paper
- A pen

- A small bowl of water
- A candle (color corresponding to your intent)

Ritual:

1. Preparation: Write your intention clearly on the paper. Use a pen that feels powerful to you.
2. **Circle Casting:** Cast a circle as desired.
3. **Invocation:** Call on any deities or spirits that resonate with your goal, or simply invoke your personal power.
4. **Charge the Intention:** Hold the piece of paper in your hands and visualize your intention coming to fruition. Feel the emotion associated with achieving it.
5. **Water Element:** Dip your fingers in the bowl of water, symbolizing the fluidity and adaptability of your desire. Say, "As water flows, so too does my intention manifest."
6. **Burning the Paper:** Carefully light the paper with the candle flame, letting it burn fully in a fire-safe dish. Visualize your intention being released into the universe as the smoke rises.
7. **Closing:** Thank any entities you called upon, extinguish the candle, and release the circle.

3. Ritual of Change and Transformation

Purpose: To facilitate personal change or transformation.

Materials:

- A piece of string or ribbon
- A small representation of what you wish to transform (e.g., a stone, a photo)
- A journal

Ritual:

1. Preparation: Write down what you wish to transform in your life in the journal.
2. **Circle Casting:** Cast a circle to create sacred space.
3. **Invocation:** Invoke energies or deities associated with change, such as Persephone or the Phoenix.
4. **Binding the Intention:** Take the string or ribbon and tie it around the representation of your transformation, saying, "I bind this intention to this symbol. Change is my will."
5. **Visualizing Change:** Hold the representation and visualize the transformation you desire. Imagine the feelings and outcomes as vividly as possible.
6. **Journaling:** Write down your feelings and insights after the visualization. Use this journal as a tool for reflection and tracking progress.
7. **Closing:** Thank any energies or deities you invoked, remove the binding, and release the circle.

4. Ritual of Chaos Sigils

Purpose: To create and charge sigils for specific outcomes.

Materials:

M Paper

M Pen

M A candle (color according to your intent)

M A quiet space

Ritual:

1. Preparation: Write your desire in a clear, concise statement (e.g., "I

am successful").
2. **Circle Casting:** Cast a circle as desired.
3. **Creation of Sigil:** Remove vowels and duplicate consonants from your statement to create a unique sigil.
4. **Charging the Sigil:** Light the candle and focus on the sigil. Visualize energy building around it. Say, "With this flame, I charge this sigil with my will."
5. **Release:** Enter a state of gnosis (e.g., through dance, drumming, or breathwork) and focus on the sigil. Let go of attachment to the outcome.
6. **Storing the Sigil:** Once charged, place the sigil somewhere you can see it or hide it away, depending on your preference for manifestation.
7. **Closing:** Thank the energies or deities you invoked and release the circle.

5. *Ritual of Integration*

Purpose: To integrate the energies and lessons learned from previous rituals.

Materials:

M A small bowl of salt

M A candle (white or black)

M Your journal

Ritual:

1. Preparation: Reflect on previous rituals and lessons. Write down key insights in your journal.
2. **Circle Casting:** Cast a circle to create sacred space.
3. **Invocation:** Call upon your higher self or spirit guides for integration and wisdom.

4. **Salt and Candle:** Sprinkle salt in a circle around the candle, symbolizing protection and grounding. Light the candle.
5. **Reflection:** Read your journal entries aloud. Allow space for contemplation and integration of these lessons.
6. **Meditation:** Meditate on the insights, allowing them to settle into your being.
7. **Closing:** Thank your higher self or guides, extinguish the candle, and release the circle.

Chapter Twelve - Various Special Rituals.

In addition to the various high holy day rituals of the 8 Sabbats - there are a variety of specialized rituals, most celebrating stages of life in one way or another. Standard sample rituals are given here for the various specialized occasions.

A **Wiccaning** is a type of blessing or naming ceremony for a child within the Wiccan or Pagan faith. It is often performed to welcome a child into the community, offer protection, and mark the beginning of their spiritual journey. This ritual can vary widely depending on personal or familial traditions, but here's a general outline for a Wiccaning ceremony:

Wiccaning Ritual: "Blessing of the Child"

Preparation

> M **Altar Setup**: Prepare an altar with items that symbolize the elements, the Goddess, and the God (candles, incense, crystals, etc.).

> " **Goddess Representation**: A statue, image, or symbol of the Goddess, such as a moon, pentacle, or chalice.

> " **God Representation**: A statue, image, or symbol of the God, such as a horned figure, pentagram, or athame (ritual knife).

> " **Elemental Representations**: Candles in the four elemental colors: red (Fire), blue (Water), green (Earth), yellow (Air).

> " **A Bowl of Water**: For cleansing and anointing.

> " **Herbs or Flowers**: For blessings and offerings.

" **A Special Blanket or Cloth**: To wrap the child in during the blessing.

" **A Name Token or Object**: A symbolic item to represent the child's name or spirit (a necklace, stone, or trinket).

▪

Participants:

M **Priest/Priestess**: The officiants of the ritual.

M **Parents/Guardians**: They will be actively involved in the naming and blessing.

M **God/Goddess Parents:** Selected friends of the parents who swear to support the parents of the child as they are raised.

M **Guests**: Friends and family of the child, who may participate in offering blessings.

The Ritual

1. Opening the Circle

" The Priest/Priestess calls upon the directions, the elements, and the divine to create sacred space. They may say something like:

2. "By the North, South, East, and West,

We call upon the Guardians of the Earth, Air, Fire, and Water.

We gather in the name of the Goddess and the God,

To bless this child and name them with love."

(Light the elemental candles, and create the circle with incense or by using a ritual tool like a wand or athame, as discussed in the last chapter.)

3. Welcoming the Child

" The Priest/Priestess or parent(s) speak words of welcome for the child. You can speak a few words about the child's birth, their spirit, or what they mean to the family.

4. "We welcome you, little one, into the light of the Goddess and God.

You are a child of the Earth, beloved and sacred.

May you grow strong in wisdom, love, and joy."

5. Naming the Child

" The parents or guardians speak the name they have chosen for the child aloud, calling upon the energies of the divine to bless this name.

6. "By the Goddess and God,

We name this child, [Child's Name],

May their spirit be as free as the wind,

As steady as the Earth,

And as radiant as the stars above."

7. Cleansing and Blessing

" The Priest/Priestess dips their fingers into the bowl of water and sprinkles a few drops on the child's forehead or gently anoints the child with the water (with parent or guardian permission). This is a symbolic cleansing and blessing.

8. "I cleanse you with the waters of life,

And bless you with purity and strength.

As you grow, may you always walk in the light."

Optionally, pass the child around to close family members or community members, who can each speak a short blessing or wish for the child's future.

9. Offering of Gifts or Blessings

" Guests may be invited to come forward and offer small tokens of good wishes, blessings, or items for the child's future. This could include herbs, crystals, charms, or written words of wisdom. These can be placed on the altar or passed directly to the child.

10. Closing the Ritual

" The Priest/Priestess closes the circle by thanking the divine, elements, and any spirits that may have been called upon during the ritual.

11. "We give thanks to the Goddess and God,

For the gift of this child and for the blessings received today.

As we leave this circle, may love and protection surround this child,

And may their path be guided by light and wisdom."

(Extinguish the candles, close the circle, and share a final moment of connection.)

12. Feasting and Celebration

" After the ritual, there can be a celebration with food, music, and socializing. It's a joyous time for family and friends to bond, offer their own support, and share in the child's blessing.

Optional Additions:

M **Elemental Blessings**: In some traditions, after the water blessing, the Priest/Priestess may light candles or speak invocations to each of the elements, asking them to guide the child's development.

M **Symbolic Object**: If using a name token or symbolic object, the child may hold it during the ceremony or it can be gifted to them as a keepsake.

M **Anointing with Oil**: In some versions of the ritual, anointing the child with blessed oil (a blend of essential oils) is used to symbolize protection and spiritual vitality.

Wiccan Coming of Age Ritual: "Rite of Passage[31]"

Preparation

M **Altar Setup**: The altar is arranged with items that symbolize the elements, the Goddess and God, and the individual's new stage in life.

" **Goddess Representation**: A symbol of the Goddess, such as a statue, chalice, or moonstone.

" **God Representation**: A symbol of the God, such as a horned figure, athame, or pentagram.

" **Candles for the Four Elements**: Red for Fire, Blue for Water, Yellow for Air, Green for Earth.

" **An Item Representing the Person**: A personal object, such as a journal, necklace, or a meaningful trinket.

" **Blessed Oil or Herb**: For anointing, symbolizing purity, wisdom, and spiritual awakening.

" **Sacred Tools**: A athame, wand, or another ritual tool that the individual has been using in their practice.

" **An Offering of Gratitude**: A gift or offering to the Earth, such as flowers, herbs, or food.

Participants:

M **The Initiate (Coming of Age Person)**: The individual marking their transition into adulthood.

M **Priest/Priestess**: The officiant or spiritual guide of the ritual.

M **Family or Community Members**: Those who may witness or participate in the ceremony, offering their support and blessings.

The Ritual

1. Opening the Circle

" The Priest/Priestess calls the quarters and invites the divine presence, ensuring that the space is sacred and protected. The individual being honored can either stand or sit at the altar.

2. "By the North, South, East, and West,

We call upon the elements,

To bless this sacred space.

By the Goddess and God,

We begin this rite of passage."

(As the directions are called, the elemental candles can be lit, and incense or other ritual tools may be used to establish the circle.)

3. Welcoming the Initiate

" The Priest/Priestess speaks words of welcome to the individual, honoring their journey to this moment and recognizing the changes they've undergone.

4. "Today, you stand at the threshold,

Between childhood and adulthood,

With the wisdom of the past,

And the promise of the future.

You are a child of the Goddess and God,

A seeker of wisdom, love, and truth."

5. Invocation of the Goddess and God

" The Priest/Priestess invokes the Goddess and God, asking them to bless the initiate with their divine guidance and protection as they move forward in life.

6. "Goddess, Mother of the Earth,

God, Father of the Sky,

We call upon your divine presence,

To guide, protect, and empower this soul.

May they walk with the wisdom of the Earth,

The fire of the Sun,

The flow of the Waters,

And the winds of the Air.As they step into the fullness of adulthood,

May they be ever true to their path."

7. The Passing of the Wisdom

" This is an important moment where the Priest/Priestess or elder figures share advice, wisdom, or blessings with the initiate. This can be done through storytelling, symbolic gestures, or offering words of encouragement for the future.

8. "The path you walk is your own,

Guided by the stars and the moon.

Know that with wisdom comes responsibility,

And with love comes growth.

Trust in yourself, and trust in the Earth.

May your steps be blessed, and your heart always true."

9. The Rite of Passage (Symbolic Actions)

" The initiate is invited to perform a symbolic act to mark their transition. This could include:

\# **Anointing with Blessed Oil**: The Priest/Priestess anoints the initiate's forehead, symbolizing spiritual awakening and readiness for the new phase of life. "As you are anointed, so may your heart, mind, and spirit be open to the wisdom of the Earth and the divine."

\# **Cleansing with Water**: The initiate may be sprinkled with sacred water, symbolizing renewal and purification.

\# **Crossing the Threshold**: If the ritual takes place outdoors or near a symbolic doorway, the initiate may be invited to step over a threshold, representing their entry into adulthood.

10. The Gift of Power or Knowledge

" The initiate is presented with a gift that symbolizes their new role. This could be a book of wisdom, a ritual tool (such as a wand or athame), a crystal, or another meaningful object that represents their spiritual journey and growth.

11. "May this [object] remind you of your power,

Your strength, and your connection to the divine.

With it, may you walk with intention,

And use your wisdom for the good of all."

12. The Oath or Promise

" The initiate may be asked to make a personal vow or promise to honor the divine, nature, and their path. This could be an affirmation of responsibility and intention.

13. "I vow to honor the Goddess and God,

To walk with wisdom, love, and respect,

To seek balance in all things,

And to honor the Earth as sacred and whole.

I step into adulthood with open arms and an open heart."

14. Closing the Ritual

" The Priest/Priestess closes the circle by thanking the divine and the elements. The initiate is congratulated and welcomed into this new phase of life with blessings for their journey ahead.

15. "By the Goddess and God,

By the elements and the Earth,

This ritual is now complete.

May you walk your path with courage and grace.

As we close this circle, we open the way for new beginnings."

(The circle is closed, and the elemental candles are extinguished.)

16. Celebration and Feasting

" After the formal part of the ritual, the group can celebrate with food, music, and community. It's a joyous occasion for all involved, with guests sharing their blessings and the initiate reflecting on the significance of the rite.

Optional Additions:

M **Sacred Dance or Song**: A song, chant, or dance that symbolizes the individual's connection to the Earth, the elements, and the divine may be performed.

M **Elemental Challenges**: A more interactive approach where the initiate faces symbolic challenges or tasks representing each of the four elements, reflecting their readiness to embody those energies [32].

M **Support of the Community**: The community can be invited to give their blessings by offering a group prayer or light (such as candles or incense).

Wiccan Handfasting Ritual[33]

Preparation

M **Altar Setup**: The altar can be decorated with symbols of the divine (the Goddess and God), the elements, and flowers.

" **Goddess Representation**: A chalice, moonstone, or Goddess figurine.

" **God Representation**: A horned God, a god figurine, or the athame.

" **Elemental Candles**: Red (Fire), Blue (Water), Yellow (Air), Green (Earth).

" **Handfasting Cord**: A ribbon or cord in colors chosen by the couple, typically 3 or 7 cords symbolizing different aspects of their union (love, trust, commitment, etc.).

" **Blessed Oil**: For anointing, symbolizing purity and connection.

" **Sacred Objects**: Items that represent the couple, such as a shared gift or object from nature.

Participants:

M **The Couple**: The individuals entering into the commitment.

M **Officiant (Priest/Priestess)**: The one leading the ceremony, calling upon the divine and elements.

M **Wedding Party:** Best man and groomsmen, Maid of Honor and Bridesmaids.

M **Guests**: Family and friends who are part of the ritual and witness the commitment.

Ritual

1. Opening the Circle

" The officiant invokes the quarters (the four directions) and calls in the divine presence to bless the sacred space.

2. "We gather here today, beneath the watchful eyes of the Goddess and God,

To bind two souls in love, commitment, and honor.

By the Earth and Sky, the Fire and Water,

We call the elements to bless this union.

Let this circle be sacred and protected."

(Light the elemental candles as each direction is invoked.)

3. Invocation of the Goddess and God

" The officiant calls upon the divine to bless the couple's union.

4. "Goddess of Love, God of Strength,

Bless this union with your sacred energies,

May the love between these two souls be nourished by your grace.

As the Moon and Sun dance together, so may their hearts be forever entwined."

5. The Declaration of Intent

" The officiant asks the couple to declare their intentions to one another, openly speaking their vows or promises.

6. "Do you, [Partner 1], take [Partner 2] as your spouse,

To walk with them in love, honor, and respect,

To share your joys, your sorrows, and your strength,

For today and all your days to come?"

(Partner 1 responds affirmatively.)

"And do you, [Partner 2], take [Partner 1] as your spouse,

To walk with them in love, honor, and respect,

To share your joys, your sorrows, and your strength,

For today and all your days to come?"

(Partner 2 responds affirmatively.)

7. Handfasting – Binding of the Hands

" The officiant takes the handfasting cords, and each cord can represent a different aspect of the relationship (e.g., red for love, yellow for communication, etc.). The officiant binds the couple's hands together with the cords, symbolizing their union.

8. "As these cords are tied, so are your hearts bound in love and commitment.

Together you will face the challenges of life, And celebrate the joy it brings, hand in hand."

(The officiant ties the couple's hands together as they each hold one end of the cord.)

9. Blessing of the Union

" The couple can exchange rings, flowers, or another item to symbolize their eternal bond.

10. "With this ring/flower, I give you my heart,

With this handfasting, I give you my soul.

We are bound in love, body and spirit,

Forevermore."

11. The Kiss and Final Blessing

" The officiant blesses the couple one last time and gives permission for the couple to kiss.

12. "By the powers of the Earth, Air, Fire, and Water,

By the love of the Goddess and God,

You are united in spirit and in heart.

Kiss now, and begin your new journey together."

(The couple kisses, and guests cheer or applaud.)

13. Closing the Circle

" The officiant thanks the elements, the divine, and the witnesses for their presence.

14. "The circle is now closed, but your union is eternal.

Go forth in love and joy, bound together by the forces of the Earth and the stars."

(The elemental candles are extinguished as the circle is closed.)

Possible Modifications for the Same-sex Couple's Ritual:

1. Opening the Circle and Invocation

" The same as the straight couple's version, but emphasizing unity between all people regardless of gender.

2. "We gather today, in the name of the Goddess and God,

To honor the sacred bond between these two souls,

Whose love transcends boundaries and brings us closer to the divine.

Let this circle be a reflection of the unity we seek in all things."

3. The Declaration of Intent

" The couple still speaks their vows to each other, with the same wording as in the straight couple's ritual. However, each vow can reflect their individual journey and unique connection.

4. Handfasting – Binding of the Hands

" The officiant uses the handfasting cords to symbolize the binding of the couple's hands and hearts. Again, this is a representation of unity and love, without the need for gender distinctions.

5. Blessing of the Union

" After the couple exchanges rings or symbolic tokens, the officiant might say:

6. "By the elements of Earth, Air, Fire, and Water,

We honor your union, bound in love and commitment.

May your hearts be free, your spirits intertwined,

In this life and the next."

7. The Kiss and Final Blessing

" As with the straight couple, the officiant gives the final blessing and the couple kisses.

8. "With this kiss, your love is sealed,

With this bond, you are united.

Walk forward hand in hand, and heart in heart,

Into the light of your shared future."

9. Closing the Circle

" The officiant closes the circle and thanks the divine for the union of the couple.

10. "By the forces of the Earth, the Moon, and the Sun,

Your bond is eternal.

May love guide you always, in all things."

Optional Modifications for Both Rituals:

M **Gender-Neutral Language**: You may choose to use language that's gender-neutral or inclusive of all orientations.

M **Community Blessings**: In either form of the ritual, the community members can come forward and offer their blessings, or the couple can invite loved ones to speak their words of support.

Eldering Rite[34]

Preparation

M **Altar Setup**: The altar should be prepared with symbols of the divine, the elements, and tools that represent wisdom, life experience, and the cycles of nature.

" **Goddess Representation**: A statue, image, or symbol of the Goddess, particularly in her Crone aspect (e.g., a dark moon, triple goddess symbol, or the Elder Mother).

" **God Representation**: A symbol of the God in his elder or wise form (e.g., the Horned God, a sage figure, or a wand).

" **Elemental Candles**: Red (Fire), Blue (Water), Yellow (Air), Green (Earth).

" **Wisdom Objects**: A book of knowledge, a staff, or a walking stick (symbolizing wisdom and the journey).

" **Candle for the Elder**: A candle dedicated to the elder's life, a white or silver candle for honoring the life they have lived.

" **Offerings**: A bowl of salt, herbs, or flowers (representing the earth and wisdom), and a cup of water or wine to symbolize the offering of sustenance and life.

" **Ritual Tools**: A staff or walking stick (if the elder has one), a chalice for the offering, and any personal items the elder would like to bring to the altar.

Participants:

M **The Elder**: The individual being honored and celebrated.

M **Priest/Priestess**: The one officiating the ritual, who will guide the ceremony and invoke the divine.

M **Community**: The family, friends, or spiritual community members who are present to witness and participate.

The Ritual

1. Opening the Circle

" The Priest/Priestess calls the quarters and invokes the divine. This sets the sacred space where the Elder can be honored by the elements and the divine energies.

2. "We gather here today, in the presence of the Goddess and God,

To honor the journey of our beloved Elder,

Who has walked the path of wisdom, love, and light.

By the elements of Earth, Air, Fire, and Water,

We call forth the sacred energies to bless this circle and this life."

(Light the elemental candles, invoking each direction, and create the circle with incense or a ritual tool.)

3. Invocation of the Goddess and God

" The Priest/Priestess invokes the divine energies to bless the Elder and the community. The Crone aspect of the Goddess and the wise Elder aspect of the God are particularly called upon in this ritual.

4. "Goddess, Crone of wisdom and time,

God, Elder of the cycles and knowledge,

We call upon you now to bless this Elder.

May their wisdom be honored, their path respected,

And their light continue to shine through us all."

5. The Elder's Life and Contributions

" The Priest/Priestess speaks of the Elder's life, their wisdom, and their contributions to the community. This can be done by the officiant or by members of the community who are invited to share stories or speak about the Elder's impact.

6. "We honor the years of knowledge you have shared,

The lessons learned and the wisdom passed down.

Your heart has guided us, your spirit has sustained us,

And your example has led us through many cycles.

Today, we celebrate you, our Elder,

And the legacy you have built."

7. The Elder's Reflection and Words of Wisdom

" The Elder is invited to share their thoughts, reflections, and wisdom with the community. This is a moment for the Elder to impart a piece of their life's lessons or a spiritual teaching.

8. "At this time, we invite you, Elder,

To share the wisdom you have gathered,

The lessons you have learned,

And the guidance you offer to the next generation. We listen with open hearts and minds."

(The Elder speaks, sharing their wisdom and reflections on their journey.)

9. The Rite of Blessing

" The Priest/Priestess takes a staff or a wand and holds it over the Elder's head, blessing them with protection, vitality, and continued wisdom. If the Elder is physically present and it feels appropriate, the Priest/Priestess might also anoint the Elder with blessed oils or water to symbolize renewal and blessing.

10. "By the power of the Earth,

By the wisdom of the Moon,

By the fire of the Sun,

And the breath of the Winds,

We bless you, Elder,

May your path continue to be filled with wisdom,

And may your years be many and rich with light."

(If oil is used, the Priest/Priestess may anoint the Elder's forehead or hands, symbolizing their ongoing spiritual guidance.)

11. The Hand of Guidance

" The Priest/Priestess or community members may offer the Elder a symbolic token of their life's work: a staff (symbolizing authority and wisdom), a book (symbolizing knowledge), or a crystal (symbolizing eternal wisdom). The Elder may hold the item, or it may be placed on the altar as a gift.

12. "This gift represents the wisdom you carry,

The knowledge you share, and the legacy you create. We offer this symbol of your life's work,

As a token of gratitude and respect."

13. The Elder's Blessing of the Community

" The Elder, now honored, is invited to bless the community in return. This can be a simple prayer, a sharing of wisdom, or an invocation of blessings upon the gathered people.

14. "May the wisdom of the ages guide you,

May the light of the stars shine upon your path,

And may you always know the love and support of the Earth.

Blessings upon each of you, now and always."

15. The Closing

" The Priest/Priestess thanks the Elder for their presence and contributions and closes the circle. The Elder's work is honored, and the community is invited to celebrate the Elder's life and wisdom.

16. "By the elements and the divine,

We close this circle, but the Elder's wisdom remains,

Ever with us, guiding and teaching.

May we honor the path they have paved,

And walk forward with gratitude in our hearts."

(The elemental candles are extinguished, and the circle is closed.)

17. **Celebration and Feast**

" After the ritual, the community gathers for a feast or gathering to celebrate the Elder, share stories, and offer personal tributes to the Elder's life and wisdom. This is a time of joy and reverence for the Elder's journey.

Optional Additions:

M **Elder's Ritual Tools**: If the Elder has specific ritual tools they've used throughout their practice, these can be presented or honored as part of the ceremony.

M **Sacred Dance or Song**: A song or dance honoring the Elder's journey or the cycles of life can be performed by the community.

M **Personal Blessings**: Community members may offer personal blessings, gifts, or tributes that reflect the impact the Elder has had on their lives.

M **A Gift of Light**: The Elder may light a candle or flame, symbolizing their enduring wisdom and the fire that continues to guide the community.

Wiccan Funeral Rites[35]

Preparation

M **Altar Setup**: The altar should reflect the sacredness of the ceremony, with items that symbolize the deceased's life, the divine, and the natural elements.

" **Candles**: White candles to symbolize the soul's journey, and black candles to honor the transition of death. The candles can also represent the four elements (Earth, Air, Fire, Water).

" **Personal Items**: Photos, personal mementos, and objects that represent the deceased's life and personality.

" **Sacred Tools**: A chalice of wine or water to represent the flow of life, incense to purify the space, and a bell to mark transitions.

" **Flowers or Earth Offerings**: To symbolize the return of the body to the Earth and the ongoing life cycle.

" **Symbolic Representation of the Elements**: For example, a small bowl of earth for grounding, a glass of water for life's flow, incense for the spirit's journey, and a small fire or flame to represent the soul's eternal flame.

Participants:

M **The Officiant (Priest/Priestess)**: The spiritual leader who guides the ritual and invokes the divine.

◼ **The Community**: Family, friends, and loved ones who have gathered to mourn the loss, honor the deceased, and offer blessings.

▪

The Ritual

1. Opening the Circle and Sacred Space

" The officiant calls the circle to create a sacred, protected space for the ceremony, invoking the elements and the divine.

2. "We gather here today, beneath the watchful eyes of the Goddess and God,

To honor and celebrate the life of [Name],

To guide them as they journey to the next stage of existence.

We call upon the elements of Earth, Air, Fire, and Water,

To hold us in this sacred space,

As we honor the passage of this soul from this life to the next."

(The officiant may light candles, incense, and a fire, invoking the four directions and the elements.)

3. Invocation of the Goddess and God

" The officiant invokes the divine presence to guide the soul of the deceased and provide comfort to the living.

4. "Goddess, Mother of all, cradle this soul in your loving arms.

God, Father of wisdom and the great cycles, guide their journey to the other side.

As they return to the great web of life,

May they find peace, love, and light in the realm of the divine."

5. The Life of the Deceased

" This is a time for family, friends, or the officiant to speak of the deceased's life, their contributions, and the ways they will be remembered. This can be done with a few words or a more detailed eulogy.

6. "We remember you, [Name], as a soul who brought light to our lives,

Your kindness, laughter, and love will never fade.

You have walked your path with courage, and now your journey continues,

With the blessing of the Goddess and God,

And the love of all who knew you."

7. Rite of Passage – Releasing the Soul

" The officiant may guide the soul on its journey to the next world by performing a symbolic act of release. This can be done by burning a written prayer, blessing, or memory, or by releasing something into the Earth, such as flowers, herbs, or a biodegradable object.

8. "As we release this offering into the Earth,

So do we release you, [Name], from the bonds of this world.

May you travel to the realm of peace,

Where love and light surround you.

May your journey be swift,

And may you find rest in the embrace of the divine."

(The officiant can offer a moment of silence for the community to reflect and send their love and blessings to the deceased.)

9. Cleansing and Purification

" A cleansing or purification ritual can be performed to purify the space and those present, ensuring that no negative energy lingers. This is often done with incense or water.

10. "By the power of the sacred smoke, we purify this space,

And cleanse our hearts of sorrow,

Releasing all attachment and holding only love,

For the spirit of [Name] is free, and we too are free."

11. The Offering of Light

" The officiant or a loved one can light a candle in the deceased's memory, symbolizing the light of the soul. A bell may be rung to signal the soul's release.

12. "As this flame burns, so does your spirit burn bright,

Guiding us with the light of your love,

And as this bell rings, so does your soul travel onward.

You are not gone, but transformed,

And forever a part of us."

13. Blessing of the Earth

" The community can be invited to participate by offering flowers or other gifts to the Earth. This symbolizes the return of the body to nature and the cycle of life.

14. "We offer this token to the Earth,

As your body returns to the ground,

So too does your spirit return to the stars,

And your essence will live on,

In the trees, the winds, and the rain."

15. **Final Blessing**

" The officiant offers a final prayer or blessing to the deceased, the family, and the community.

16. "May the Goddess and God watch over you,

As you travel to the other side,

And may you rest in peace and love.

We honor you now, and we honor you always,

Until we meet again in the next life.

So mote it be."

(Guests may be invited to come forward and offer personal tributes, prayers, or blessings to the deceased.)

17. **Closing the Circle**

" The officiant closes the circle by thanking the elements, the divine, and the deceased's spirit for their presence.

18. "The circle is now closed,

The space sacred and complete,

But the love of [Name] will never leave,

And the bond of our hearts will endure.

Blessed be."

(The candles are extinguished, and the ritual is complete.)

Optional Additions:

M **Sacred Song or Chant**: A song or chant can be performed to honor the deceased, such as a hymn or a song of remembrance.

M **Symbolic Actions**: Family and friends can participate by placing flowers, herbs, or mementos on the altar or grave, symbolizing their love and remembrance.

M **Memorial Tree or Planting**: In some Wiccan traditions, a tree or plant may be planted in the memory of the deceased, representing the continuation of life and the cycle of nature.

The Wiccan approach to death is rooted in the belief that life is cyclical, and death is merely a transition. These rites are focused on guiding the soul to the next realm with love, honoring the deceased's journey, and celebrating their life. The rituals help the community move through their grief while affirming the belief in eternal connection and the continuous cycle of life, death, and rebirth.

Chapter Thirteen – Occasional Rituals

Blessing of the Hearth and Home

Preparation

> M **Altar Setup**: Prepare a small altar in the center of the home or a space where the ritual can begin (e.g., the living room or hearth).
>
> " **Candles**: White or gold candles to represent purity and light, and colored candles for specific blessings (e.g., green for prosperity, pink for love, blue for peace).
>
> " **Salt**: A small dish of salt, which is used for purification and grounding.
>
> " **Water**: A small bowl of water, representing cleansing and the flow of life.
>
> " **Herbs**: Fresh herbs (such as sage, rosemary, or thyme) for purification, or incense to purify the space.
>
> " **Pentacle**: A pentacle or other symbol representing protection.
>
> " **Bell or Chime**: A bell or chime to mark transitions and summon good energy.
>
> " **Flowers**: A bouquet of flowers, especially roses, or any plant that represents growth, beauty, and renewal.

Participants:

> M **Homeowner(s)**: The individual or family seeking the blessing.
>
> M **Officiant (Priest/Priestess)**: The person leading the ceremony, invoking the elements and the divine.

The Ritual

1. Opening the Circle

" The officiant creates a sacred space by invoking the quarters and calling in the elements. The intention is to establish a protective boundary around the home and invite the divine into the space.

2. "We stand here today, in this space we call home,

And we ask the sacred elements to come and bless us.

May the Earth bring us grounding,

May the Air bring us clarity,

May the Fire bring us passion and warmth,

May the Water bring us healing and flow.

We ask the divine, Goddess and God, to bless this space with love, light, and peace."

(Light the candles for each direction, and ring the bell or chime to signal the beginning of the ritual.)

3. Cleansing the Space

" Begin by walking around the house with the salt, water, or herbs/incense to cleanse the space of any lingering negative or stagnant energy. As you walk, speak words of purification.

4. "I cast out all energies that no longer serve this space,

And welcome only love, light, and peace.

WHY WICCA

By the Earth's grounding power, I purify this home,

By the Air's breath, I clear away all negativity,

By the Fire's flame, I banish all darkness,

And by the Water's flow, I bring healing and peace."

(Sprinkle salt or lightly anoint water in each room, or burn herbs/incense and wave the smoke through the space, moving clockwise to represent positive energy flow.)

5. Calling in Divine Blessings

" The officiant calls upon the divine for protection, harmony, and blessings within the home. A prayer or invocation is made to honor the divine and invite them into the home.

6. "Goddess, I invite your nurturing presence,

Fill this home with love, compassion, and harmony.

God, I invite your strength and protection,

Guard this space with your steady hand and guidance.

May this home be filled with warmth, peace, and abundance,

May all who enter here feel safe, welcomed, and loved."

7. Invoking the Elements and Blessing Specific Areas

" In this part of the ritual, each room of the house can be blessed for specific purposes (e.g., prosperity, love, peace). You can move from room to room, dedicating each space to specific intentions, and use the elements to bless each space.

8. **Living Room** (Peace and Harmony):

"May this room be filled with peace, laughter, and friendship.

May all who enter here find solace and joy."

Kitchen (Health and Nourishment):

"May this kitchen be a place of nourishment,

A place where health, vitality, and abundance flow."

Bedroom (Love and Rest):

"May this bedroom be filled with restful sleep and love.

May all who sleep here find comfort and renewal."

Workspace or Office (Prosperity and Creativity):

"May this space be filled with creativity, focus, and prosperity.

May all who work here find success and abundance."

Hallways and Entrances (Protection and Welcome):

"May all who enter this home feel welcomed,

May this space be guarded and protected from harm."

(Move around the house with the bell or chime, blessing each area with words of intention. You can also sprinkle salt, water, or incense in each space as you go.)

9. Offering of Flowers and Final Blessing

" The homeowner(s) can place flowers in the center of the altar or at the front door to symbolize growth, new beginnings, and the blessings of nature. A final prayer or blessing is offered for the household.

10. "As the flowers bloom, may peace, love, and prosperity bloom within this home.

As we step forward into this space, may we do so with light hearts and open minds.

We are blessed by the divine and the elements,

And this home is now a sacred place of love, peace, and joy.

Blessed be this house, this family, and all who dwell within.

So mote it be."

11. **Closing the Circle**

" The officiant closes the circle, thanking the elements and the divine for their protection and blessings.

12. "We give thanks to the elements,

To the Goddess and God,

For their presence and protection.

The circle is now closed,

But the blessings continue to flow,

Throughout this home and all who dwell here.

So mote it be."

(Extinguish the candles, and the ritual is complete.)

Optional Additions:

- **Chant or Song**: A song or chant may be sung to further invoke positive energy and fill the home with a loving vibration. A simple chant such as "Blessed be, this home we see, filled with love and harmony," might be used.

- **Blessing of the Threshold**: The entrance of the home may be blessed with salt, water, or herbs, as the threshold represents the boundary between the outside world and the sacred space of the home.

- **Crystal or Gemstone Ritual**: A crystal or gemstone (e.g., amethyst for peace, citrine for prosperity, rose quartz for love) may be placed in each room or in a central location to amplify the intentions of the ritual.

Blessing of Prosperity and Success for a Business

Preparation:

- **Altar Setup**: A small altar can be placed in the center of the business space or an important room (e.g., the main office or storefront). The altar should contain symbols representing prosperity, abundance, and the elements.

- **Candles**: Green (prosperity), gold (success), and white (purity and protection) candles.

- **Crystals**: Citrine (abundance), pyrite (prosperity), or aventurine (growth) crystals placed on the altar.

- **Coins or Bills**: Representing wealth and prosperity, to be offered during the ritual.

- **Incense**: Cinnamon, frankincense, or patchouli incense for abundance and positive energy.

" **Small Offering**: A small bowl of salt (purification) or water (flow of energy) to cleanse the space.

" **Symbol of the Business**: A logo, name card, or something symbolic of the business.

" **Flowers**: Fresh flowers to represent growth and new beginnings.

Participants:

M **Business Owner(s)**: The individual(s) seeking the blessing for their business.

M **Officiant (Priest/Priestess)**: The one guiding the ritual.

M **Community or Friends**: If desired, family or friends can participate in the ceremony to offer their support and blessings.

The Ritual

1. Opening the Circle and Sacred Space

" The officiant begins by casting a circle to create a sacred space, invoking the elements and the divine. The circle sets the space apart from the mundane and opens the energy to divine blessings.

2. "We gather here today to bless this space,

This business that is new,

May it grow with strength and abundance,

And flourish with love, light, and prosperity.

By the elements of Earth, Air, Fire, and Water,

We call the sacred energies to surround this place,

And to guide all who enter here with wisdom, grace, and success."

(Light the candles and incense to represent each of the elements. Walk around the space with the incense, sprinkling salt, or purifying with water as you call in each direction: North (Earth), East (Air), South (Fire), and West (Water).)

3. **Invocation of the Goddess and God**

" The officiant invokes the divine feminine and masculine energies to bless the business and its growth. This can be adapted depending on the pantheon or deities you work with.

4. "Goddess of abundance, of harvest and prosperity,

We invite you into this space.

May your divine blessings fill this business,

And bring it fruitful growth and lasting success.

God of wisdom, of strength and protection,

We ask that you guide and support the ventures of this business,

May your light shine upon all who work here and enter this space."

5. **Blessing of the Business Space**

" The officiant walks around the business space (or each room of the business), speaking blessings for prosperity, protection, and success. Each area should be blessed to invite positive energy and align the space with the business's goals.

For the Entryway:

"May all who enter this place find abundance and opportunity,

May they feel welcome, valued, and energized.

May this business be a beacon of light,

Attracting customers, clients, and growth."

For the Office or Workspace:

"May this space be filled with clarity, focus, and creativity,

May the work here be guided by wisdom and joy,

And may success come easily to those who labor here."

For the Retail or Sales Floor:

"May this space be abundant with opportunities,

May the goods and services offered here be blessed,

And may prosperity flow easily to this business."

(As you move through the space, use the bell or chime to mark the energy shifts, or anoint corners of rooms with salt or water to cleanse and purify. Optionally, place crystals in key areas for amplified positive energy.)

6. **Offering of Prosperity**

" The business owner(s) place a token of prosperity on the altar, such as coins, bills, or a small offering of fruit or food, as a symbolic gesture of welcoming abundance and success into the business.

7. "With this offering, we invite prosperity to flow freely here,

May wealth and abundance come easily and frequently,

May this business thrive and grow,

In abundance, wisdom, and love."(The business owner(s) may speak personal intentions or desires for the business's future at this time.)

8. Blessing of Protection

" After the space has been blessed for prosperity, the officiant offers a prayer or chant to protect the business and its owners from negativity, competition, or obstacles.

9. "Goddess and God, protect this space,

Keep it free from harm and negativity,

May all those who enter here feel safe and supported,

And may any barriers to success be removed.

Protect this business from ill-willed energy,

And guide its path with strength and wisdom."

(Use a small bell or chime to symbolize the clearing of negative energy, and walk around the space again, creating a protective shield with your intentions and words.)

10. Closing the Ritual

" The officiant closes the ritual by thanking the divine, the elements, and the energies that have been invoked, ensuring that the business is spiritually aligned for success and prosperity.

11. "We give thanks to the Goddess and God,

To the elements and to the divine,

For the abundance, prosperity, and protection that we've called into this space.

We know that with their blessings, this business will grow strong and successful,

May it flourish, may it thrive, and may it always be filled with light.

The circle is now closed,But the energy of abundance remains.

So mote it be."

(Extinguish the candles and offer a moment of silence for reflection.)

Optional Additions:

M **Crystal Grid**: Create a crystal grid within the business space (or a specific room) to amplify the blessings. Place stones of prosperity (e.g., citrine, pyrite, green aventurine) in key locations, such as near the cash register, workspace, or areas where clients interact with the business.

M **Blessing of Tools**: If the business involves specific tools or equipment (e.g., a desk, instruments, or products), they can be anointed with essential oils, blessed with water, or placed under the altar for a specific blessing.

M **Chant or Song**: A chant or song of prosperity, such as "Abundance flows to me, prosperity will always be," can be sung to further raise the energy and vibration of the space

Fatherhood and Motherhood Rituals

Wiccan Ritual to Honor Fatherhood

(A Ritual for the Father on the Birth of His Child)

Preparation:

M **Altar Setup**: Set up an altar with items symbolizing the father's role, strength, and the child's arrival.

" **Candles**: Blue for wisdom, strength, and protection; gold for success and guidance.

" **Crystals**: Carnelian or tiger's eye for strength, vitality, and protection.

" **Symbols of Fatherhood**: A small item representing the father's role, such as a hand-carved token or a small gift for the child.

" **Herbs/Incense**: Cedar for protection, rosemary for remembrance, and sandalwood for wisdom.

" **A small bowl of water**: Symbolizing the flow of life, growth, and nourishment.

" **A small bowl of earth or salt**: Representing stability, grounding, and the father's protective role.

" **A bell or chime**: To mark significant moments during the ritual.

Participants:

M **Father**: The person being honored.

M **Officiant (Priest/Priestess)**: The person leading the ritual[36].

M **Family and Close Friends**: Those who wish to support and honor the new father.

The Ritual

1. **Opening the Circle**
   The officiant creates a sacred space and invites the divine to be present in the moment.
   "We gather here today to honor and celebrate the new life that is entering this world, and the new father who is stepping into his role. By the power of the elements—Earth, Air, Fire, and Water—we open this circle, a sacred space to bring forth love, light, and guidance. May the blessings of the God and Goddess surround us, as we honor the strength, wisdom, and protection that the father will offer to his new child."
   (Light candles for the elements, starting with the Earth candle for grounding, then Air, Fire, and Water.)

1. **Invocation of the God (Father Archetype)**
   The officiant calls upon the divine masculine energy to bless the father.
   *"We call upon the God, the Father, the provider and protector,
   Guide and guardian of all that is male,
   We ask for your blessings upon this father,
   May he be wise in his teachings, strong in his protection,
   And loving in his embrace.
   May he honor his new child with strength and gentleness,
   And may his role as protector and guide be forever blessed."*
   (The father may hold the water bowl, symbolizing the nourishing role he will play, while being honored for his masculine strength and protective spirit.)

1. **Blessing the Father's Role**
   The officiant gives a blessing for the father's new journey.
   *"As the sun shines brightly in the sky,
   May your heart and strength grow ever brighter.
   May you be grounded as the mighty oak,
   Rooted in your love, guidance, and protection.
   You are now the guardian of a new soul, A father who will shape and guide,*

A teacher, a protector, a nurturer of dreams."
(The father may be asked to place his hands on the earth or salt bowl, symbolizing his new role as the grounded foundation of his family.)

1. **Cleansing and Protection**
   The father may be sprinkled with water to cleanse and bless him in his new role.
   "By this water, we cleanse and bless you,
   May you be pure in your role as father,
   May this water wash away doubts and fears,
   And fill you with clarity, strength, and protection.
   You walk forward now with wisdom and courage."
   (The father is gently sprinkled with the water as the officiant offers this blessing.)

1. **Final Blessing**
   The officiant offers a final prayer for the father and the family.
   "May your journey into fatherhood be one of joy, growth, and abundance.
   May you always be a steady rock, full of love, guidance, and protection.
   May your bond with your child grow ever strong and filled with light,
   And may you find peace in your new role.
   Blessed be, father, in your strength, wisdom, and love."

1. **Closing the Circle**
   The officiant closes the circle with gratitude and thanks.
   "The circle is now closed, But the blessings of the God and Goddess continue to shine upon this father and child,
   May their lives be filled with love, laughter, and strength,
   So mote it be."

Wiccan Ritual to Honor Motherhood

(A Ritual for the Mother on the Birth of Her Child)

Preparation:

M **Altar Setup**: Set up an altar with items that symbolize motherhood, nurturing, and the new child.

" **Candles**: Pink for love, nurturing, and compassion; green for growth and harmony; and white for purity and protection.

" **Crystals**: Rose quartz for love, moonstone for fertility and nurturing, and jade for health and abundance.

" **Herbs/Incense**: Lavender for peace and calm, rose for love, and frankincense for spiritual connection.

" **A small bowl of water**: To symbolize the flow of life and nourishment.

" **A small bowl of earth or salt**: Representing the mother's grounding energy.

" **Symbol of the Child**: A small blanket, a piece of baby clothing, or a gift for the child.

Participants:

M **Mother**: The person being honored.

M **Officiant (Priest/Priestess)**: The person leading the ritual[35].

M **Family and Close Friends**: Those who wish to support and honor the new mother.

The Ritual

1. **Opening the Circle**
   The officiant creates a sacred space for honoring the new mother and child.
   "We gather here today to honor the new life that has entered this world, and the mother who will guide, protect, and nurture. We call upon the divine energies of the Goddess, the Mother of all creation, to bless this mother and child. By the power of the Earth, Air, Fire, and Water, we open this circle of love, light, and protection."
   (Light candles for the elements, starting with the Earth candle for nurturing, then Air, Fire, and Water.)

2. **Invocation of the Goddess (Mother Archetype)**
   The officiant calls upon the divine feminine energy to bless the mother.
   "We call upon the Goddess, Mother of all life,
   Nurturer, protector, and source of love.
   Bless this mother with your grace,
   May she nurture and guide this child with your strength and wisdom,
   May she be filled with unconditional love,
   And may her bond with her child be a reflection of your sacred love."
   (The mother may hold the bowl of water, symbolizing the nourishment she will provide for her child, both physically and emotionally.)

3. **Blessing the Mother's Role**
   The officiant gives a blessing to honor the mother's new journey.
   "As the moon's light shines upon the Earth,
   So does your love shine upon your child.
   May your heart be as vast as the ocean, May your hands be gentle and strong,
   You are the nurturer of dreams,
   The keeper of this child's heart,
   May your path as a mother be full of love, light, and grace."

(The mother may be asked to place her hands on the earth or salt bowl to symbolize her grounding energy and nurturing role.)

1. **Cleansing and Blessing**
   The mother may be gently anointed with water as a symbol of her sacred role.
   "By this water, we cleanse and bless you,
   May you be filled with love, patience, and peace,
   May this water wash away any fears or doubts,
   And bless you with clarity, strength, and grace.
   You walk forward now in love and light,
   A mother, strong and full of nurturing power."
   (Gently sprinkle the mother with water or anoint her hands, symbolizing her sacred motherhood.)

1. **Final Blessing**
   The officiant offers a final prayer for the mother and child.
   "May your journey into motherhood be one of joy, peace, and abundance,
   May your love grow stronger with each passing day,
   May you always find strength and comfort in your role as mother,
   And may your bond with your child be unbreakable and eternal.
   Blessed be, mother, in your love, wisdom, and grace."

1. **Closing the Circle**
   The officiant closes the circle with gratitude.
   "The circle is now closed,
   But the blessings of the Goddess continue to fill this mother and child,
   May their lives be filled with love, peace, and abundance.
   So mote it be."

Optional Additions:

M **Handfasting of Parenthood**: A symbolic "handfasting" ritual can be done between the parents to honor their partnership in this new stage of life.

M **Family Participation**: Involve family members or close friends in the ceremony, where each can offer a blessing, prayer, or gift to the parents and child.

M **Gift Blessing**: Place any gifts for the parents or child on the altar and offer blessings for them.

Wiccan Hand-Parting[37] Ritual[38]

Preparation:

M **Altar Setup**: A simple altar is set up, with candles and symbols representing closure, healing, and new beginnings. You may want to include:

" **Candles**: White or lavender for peace and healing, or blue for calm and release.

" **Crystals**: Amethyst for healing, rose quartz for compassion, and clear quartz for clarity.

" **Symbols of the Relationship**: Items that represent the partnership (photos, letters, keepsakes), which can be placed on the altar.

" **A String or Ribbon**: To represent the bond between the two individuals. The ribbon should be long enough to be tied around both individuals' hands.

" **Herbs/Incense**: Lavender for calm, sage for purification, or frankincense for spiritual clarity and healing.

" **A Small Bowl of Water**: For cleansing and renewal.

" **Salt**: For purification.

" **Paper and Pen**: For writing intentions or thoughts that need to be released.

" **A Bell or Chime**: To mark transitions and moments of release.

" **A Small Bowl or Vessel**: To place the ribbon or items of the relationship into at the end of the ritual.

Participants:

M **Two Individuals**: The individuals involved in the hand-parting.

M **Officiant**: A trusted person to guide the ritual and witness the process. Generally should be a priest or priestess.

The Ritual

1. **Opening the Circle**
   The officiant begins by creating a sacred space. The purpose of this is to protect the energies and create a container for the ceremony's intentions.
   "We gather here today, not to separate in sorrow, but to honor the time we have shared,
   To give thanks for the love, the lessons, and the growth we have experienced together.
   We call upon the elements—Earth, Air, Fire, and Water—to support us in this transition,
   And to help us move forward with peace, clarity, and grace."
   (Light the candles and incense, and walk around the space, inviting the energy of each direction. The officiant should lead the walk,

but the individuals involved should follow.)

1. **Invocation of Divine Support**
   The officiant invokes the divine (Goddess and God, or any deity the individuals feel connected to) to bless the ritual.
   "Goddess of healing, God of strength,
   We call upon your support in this time of change.
   May our hearts be open to healing,
   May our spirits be guided toward peace,
   As we release what no longer serves us,
   And walk toward new beginnings."

1. **Sharing of Intentions**
   The participants, if comfortable, may choose to speak their intentions for the ritual. Each may express what they are letting go of, what they are grateful for, and what they wish to receive moving forward. This can be done as a personal prayer or as spoken words of intention.
   "I release the bond we have held,
   I honor the love we shared,
   And I ask for healing and clarity as I move forward.
   May this parting bring peace to both of us,
   And may we each find our own path to growth and fulfillment."

1. **Binding of Hands (Symbolic Representation of the Bond)**
   The participants each take a length of ribbon, string, or cord, which represents the bond they once shared. They each hold one end of the ribbon and bring it together in the middle, tying it around their hands. The ribbon can be tied loosely, symbolizing the connection that once existed, but now is being released.
   "As we tie this ribbon, we honor our shared time,
   But we acknowledge that we must now part, The bond that once held us together is now loosened,
   And we free ourselves to walk our own paths."

1. **Cleansing and Releasing**
   The officiant sprinkle the ribbon, the hands, or the space with a small amount of water and/or salt to purify and cleanse the energy of the relationship. If using a small bowl of water, they can dip the ribbon or hands into the water to symbolize cleansing.
   "By the water's flow, we cleanse ourselves,
   May this bond be purified, and its lessons remain in our hearts.
   May this water bring healing, renewal, and peace,
   As we release what no longer serves us."

1. **Writing and Release**
   The participants are invited to write down any lingering thoughts, emotions, or memories that they need to release. After writing, they may choose to either burn the paper in a fireproof dish or bury it in the earth, releasing it symbolically.
   "I release these thoughts and feelings,
   I let them go,
   And as I release them into the fire (or earth),
   I release the past,
   So I may move forward in peace."
   (The officiant offers words of support and acknowledgment.)

1. **Severing of the Bond (Hand-Parting)**
   The officiant takes a pair of scissors to sever the ribbon or cord. The cutting of the ribbon symbolizes the final release of the relationship and the cutting of energetic ties that no longer serve the individuals. Together the following is recited:
   "By this cut, we sever the bond once shared,
   And we walk forward separately, but in peace,
   May we both find our own paths to healing and growth,
   And may we always honor the lessons we've learned from each other."

2. **Final Blessing and Healing**
   The officiant offers a final blessing, sending wishes of peace, healing, and new beginnings.
   "May we each walk forward in our own strength,

May our hearts be open to love, and our paths full of clarity,
We honor the time we shared,
And now, we release it with love and gratitude.
May the God and Goddess bless our journeys,
And guide us to where we are meant to be.
Blessed be."

1. **Closing the Circle**
   The officiant closes the circle, thanking the elements and divine energy for their presence and support.
   "The circle is now closed,
   The energies of release and healing continue,
   As we part with grace and gratitude,
   And move forward in peace.
   So mote it be."
   (Extinguish the candles and bell or chime to signify the end of the ritual.)

Optional Additions:

M **Healing Touch**: After the hand-parting, participants can place their hands on each other's shoulders or hands as a gesture of mutual respect and healing. This can help to soften the transition and mark a final moment of shared peace.

M **Gift Exchange**: If appropriate, the individuals may exchange a final small token or gift as a sign of respect for their time together.

M **Personal Prayer or Affirmation**: Each participant may close with a personal prayer, affirmation, or intention for their future healing, growth, and new path ahead.

To Sanctify a Sacred Space for Worship

This ritual is designed to permanently sanctify a space for worship, such as a Wiccan meeting hall or church, and to dedicate it as a place of spiritual connection, healing, and growth. The sanctification should invite the presence of the Divine, bless the space with protective energies, and create a safe, harmonious environment for all who enter. It is a ceremony of intention, protection, and reverence.

Preparation:

> M **Altar Setup**: A central altar can be created, ideally placed in a prominent location within the space. It may include:
>
> " **Candles**: White for purity, green for growth, and gold for spiritual illumination.
>
> " **Crystals**: Clear quartz to amplify energy, selenite for purification, amethyst for spiritual connection, and black tourmaline for protection.

- **Herbs/Incense:** Sage or palo santo for purification, frankincense or myrrh for divine connection, and lavender for peace.

- **Bowls of Water and Salt:** For purification, healing, and protection.

- **Bells or Chimes:** To mark sacred moments and transitions within the ritual.

- **Symbol of the Divine:** Statues or pictures of the God and Goddess, or other divine representations important to the congregation.

- **Offerings:** A small offering of gratitude, such as fresh flowers, fruit, or a symbolic item that represents the intentions of the space (e.g., a small bell, candle, or piece of art).

- **Space Preparation:** Clean and tidy the space physically to reflect the sanctity of the ritual. This could involve sweeping, dusting, and anointing key areas with sacred water or oils to purify them.

Participants:

- **Congregation or Group:** Those involved in the worship and spiritual activities within the space.

- **Officiant:** Priest/Priestess or Priest OR Priestess

M **Community Members**: Anyone who wishes to participate in the blessing, whether they are the leaders or members of the congregation.

The Ritual

1. Opening the Circle and Invocation of the Elements The officiants begins by establishing sacred space, ensuring that the area is protected and surrounded by the divine.

"We gather here today in the sacredness of this space,

To dedicate it to the Divine, to the God and Goddess,

May this place be a refuge for all who seek wisdom, peace, and connection.

By the power of the Four Sacred Elements—Earth, Air, Fire, and Water—we invite the energies of purification, protection, and spiritual presence into this place.

As we open this circle, we call upon the spirits of this space to be our allies, guiding us into the Light of Divine Truth."

(The officiant(s) light(s) the candles and incense, and walks around the space, invoking each direction, calling on the powers of Earth, Air, Fire, and Water to bless the space.)

" **North (Earth)**: "By the power of the Earth, we ground this space in protection and stability. May this place be a solid foundation for spiritual work and growth."

" **East (Air)**: "By the power of Air, we call forth clarity, wisdom, and communication, so that all who enter here may find insight and truth."

" **South (Fire)**: "By the power of Fire, we ignite the flame of divine inspiration and passion, that all who enter may find light in the darkness and strength in the trials of life."

" **West (Water)**: "By the power of Water, we bring peace, emotional healing, and intuition to this space, so that all who come here may be cleansed and made whole."

2. **Invocation of the Divine (God and Goddess)** The officiant(s) calls upon the God and Goddess to bless the space and consecrate it as a sacred place for worship.

"Great Goddess, who dwells in the Moon, the Earth, and the Waters,

And God, who shines through the Sun, the Stars, and the Fire,

We call upon your sacred energies,

To bless and sanctify this space for the highest good.

May your presence fill this hall with love, light, and protection,

May this place be a sanctuary for all who come to seek wisdom, healing, and connection.

We dedicate this space to you, and to the work of the divine in this world."

(The officiant may light a special candle, anoint the altar, or hold a symbolic gesture to call in the presence of the Divine.)

3. **Purification of the Space** The space is cleansed of any residual negative energy, old emotions, or imbalances. This can be done through the burning of sage or palo santo, or by sprinkling salt water throughout the space.

"By the sacred smoke of sage (or palo santo),

We purify this space, and all who enter it,

May all negative energies and unwanted influences be released and transformed.

We ask that this space be made clear, open, and receptive to Divine Light."

(The officiant(s) walk(s) around the space with the smoke, or sprinkles water in the corners of the room, while the participants may focus on the purification process, imagining any remaining negativity being cleansed.)

4. **Consecration of the Space** The officiant(s) may now consecrate the altar and the entire space by anointing key areas with a sacred oil or water. This is done to symbolize the physical and spiritual sanctification of the space.

"We anoint this altar (and this space) with sacred oil/water,

To consecrate it as a holy place of worship,

May it always be filled with divine light,

May the energies here be positive and harmonious,

And may this space serve as a beacon for those seeking spiritual fulfillment, wisdom, and community."

(As the officiant(s) anoint(s) the altar and corners of the room with water or oil, the participants may visualize the space glowing with divine light and protection.)

5. **Offerings to the Divine** Offerings are presented to honor the God and Goddess and give thanks for the

space and its purpose. These offerings can be flowers, fruit, candles, or any symbol of gratitude.

"We give thanks for the blessings of this space,

And offer these gifts to you,

May this space always be filled with your love,

And may it be a place of healing, growth, and connection for all who enter."

(The offerings are placed on the altar or another designated area. The participants can then join in a moment of silent gratitude.)

6. Invocation of the Sacred Intentions of the Space

The officiant(s) invite(s) the community to speak aloud or silently their intentions for the space and what they hope to achieve in this sacred hall (Each participant may either speak their personal intention for the space aloud or hold their intention in their heart.) and then intones.

"May this place be a sanctuary for peace and healing,

May it be a temple of wisdom and love,

May it be a home for all those seeking light, truth, and understanding.

May it always be filled with the energy of harmony, prosperity, and community."

10. **Final Blessing and Protection** The officiant(s) close(s) the ritual with a final blessing, asking for the continuous protection and divine guidance of the space.

"By the power of the Divine, we bless and protect this space,

May it always remain a sanctuary of love, truth, and peace,

May it be a place where the God and Goddess dwell,

And may it be a source of healing, light, and wisdom for all who enter.

As we leave this circle, we take with us the sacredness of this space,

And we honor it with every step we take.

Blessed be, this sacred space is now consecrated."

(The officiant(s) extinguish(es) the candles and sounds bell or chimes to mark the closing of the ritual.)

Optional Additions:

M **Blessing of the Congregation**: The officiant may offer a final blessing to all present, asking that each person leave with the peace, wisdom, and protection of the sacred space in their hearts.

M **Crystal Grid**: If desired, a crystal grid can be set up in the space to amplify the sanctification, with stones representing prosperity, protection, spiritual connection, and healing.

Ritual Tools[39]

There are ten (10) common ritual objects used in Wicca and there may be other ritual objects used by some groups (the crystal matrix, with its buried crystals in New Aeon is an excellent example of an additional tool or ritual object). These tools are traditionally blessed before being used, or in some cases, like the matrix, "attuned" to the group.

The ten most common tools, and their purposes are as follows:

1. Athame

> M **Description**: A double-edged ritual knife, traditionally with a black handle.
>
> M **Purpose**: Symbolizes the element of Air (in some traditions Fire). Used to direct energy, cast circles, and cut energetic cords—not for physical cutting.
>
> M **Why**: Represents will, power, and intention.

2. Wand

> M **Description**: Usually made of wood, sometimes adorned with crystals or metal.
>
> M **Purpose**: Directs energy in a gentler way than the athame. Used to invoke deities, draw symbols in the air, or stir energy.

M **Why**: Symbolizes the element of Air (or Fire, depending on tradition). Represents communication and spiritual direction.

3. Chalice

M **Description**: A cup or goblet, often made of silver, brass, or ceramic.

M **Purpose**: Holds water or wine for ritual, used in the symbolic Great Rite.

M **Why**: Symbolizes the element of Water and the divine feminine.

4. Pentacle

M **Description**: A disc or plate engraved with a five-pointed star within a circle.

M **Purpose**: Used to consecrate tools, hold offerings, or anchor energies on the altar.

M **Why**: Symbolizes Earth, protection, and the material world.

5. Cauldron

M **Description**: A small pot, often cast iron.

M **Purpose**: Used for burning incense, holding water, or mixing ritual ingredients. Can also represent transformation and rebirth.

- **Why**: Symbolizes the element of Water or Fire, and the womb of the Goddess.

6. Censer or Incense Burner

- **Description**: A vessel to burn incense, may be a hanging censer or simple dish.

- **Purpose**: Used to purify the space, represent Air, and carry prayers.

- **Why**: Symbolizes the element of Air and is linked to breath and spirit.

7. Bell

- **Description**: A small bell or chime.

- **Purpose**: Used to clear energy, mark the beginning or end of rituals, or invoke spirits or deities.

- **Why**: Associated with Air and vibration; believed to drive away negative energies.

8. Boline

- **Description**: A white-handled knife, often curved.

- **Purpose**: Used for physical tasks such as cutting herbs, cords, or carving candles.

- **Why**: Practical counterpart to the athame; connects magical practice to the physical world.

9. Broom (Besom)

- **Description**: A traditional broom made from natural materials.

- **Purpose**: Sweeps away negative energy; can be used to symbolically "sweep" the circle before a ritual.

- **Why**: Symbolizes cleansing and preparation; also used in handfasting ceremonies.

10. Book of Shadows

- **Description**: A personal journal or grimoire.

- **Purpose**: Contains rituals, magical usages, correspondences, and personal reflections.

- **Why**: Records your magical journey; a sacred tool of knowledge and continuity.

Ceremony to Bless the Ritual Objects

1. Cast the Circle

- Walk clockwise around the space, holding your athame or wand, saying:

"I cast this circle to create sacred space. Let no harm enter, let only love remain."

2. Call the Elements

M Face each direction and say:

" "Spirits of the East, powers of Air, I call you to bless this rite."

" "Spirits of the South, powers of Fire, I call you to bless this rite."

" "Spirits of the West, powers of Water, I call you to bless this rite."

" "Spirits of the North, powers of Earth, I call you to bless this rite."

3. Invoke the Divine

M Say:

"Goddess and God, Lord and Lady, I invite you to witness this consecration and bless these tools."

4. Consecrate Each Tool

M Take each tool one at a time and pass it through or touch it to the four elements:

" **Air** (Incense): "I cleanse and bless you with the element of Air."

" **Fire** (Candle): "I cleanse and bless you with the element of Fire."

" **Water** (Bowl): "I cleanse and bless you with the element of Water."

" **Earth** (Salt or soil): "I cleanse and bless you with the element of Earth."

M Then hold the tool to your heart and say:

"May you serve me well in my workings. I bless you in the name of the God and Goddess. So mote it be."

5. Close the Circle

M Thank the elements in reverse order (North to East).

M Say:

"The circle is open but unbroken. May the peace of the Goddess go in my heart. Merry meet, merry part, and merry meet again."

Chapter Fourteen – Wiccan Apologetics

I. Introduction: What Is Apologetics?

To many modern ears, the word *apologetics* may sound like an apology, an admission of guilt or wrongdoing. But in its oldest and truest sense, the word means something quite different. Derived from the Greek word *apologia*, it refers to a reasoned defense—a careful, thoughtful explanation of one's beliefs. It is not a plea for forgiveness, but a standing of one's ground with wisdom, compassion, and clarity.

In many religious traditions, apologetics has served as a bridge—between the faithful and the skeptical, between the misunderstood and those who misunderstand. In the Christian world, apologetics has been a robust discipline for centuries, answering criticisms and articulating doctrine to both believers and non-believers. The same can be said of Islamic, Jewish, Buddhist, and even secular humanist thought.

Wicca, as a modern Pagan religion, has rarely had that same privilege. Though its followers are many and its roots deep, Wicca has often been forced into the margins—misrepresented in media, misunderstood by the public, and mistaken for something it is not. For this reason, the practice of Wiccan apologetics is not about conversion or confrontation. It is not about defending dogma. It is about *bearing witness*—speaking truthfully and calmly about a path that is sacred, beautiful, and too often maligned.

Wiccan apologetics means learning to explain—not to justify. It means being able to speak clearly and peacefully when someone asks, "So... what exactly do you believe?" It means being grounded enough to answer suspicion with wisdom, and secure enough to meet hostility with dignity.

This chapter is an invitation. It calls us to step forward—not to argue, but to share. Not to defend ourselves with anger, but to offer understanding in a world that often misunderstands. Apologetics is not a shield; it is a lantern. And in a world still lit by misinformation and fear, even a small light can make a path easier to walk.

II. Why Wicca Needs Apologetics Today

Wicca walks a curious line in the modern world. On the one hand, it has gained visibility like never before. It appears in novels, films, television, and social media, often cloaked in mystery or flair. On the other hand, this visibility does not always translate to understanding. For every respectful portrayal, there are a dozen misrepresentations. For every sincere question, there may be suspicion, ridicule, or dismissal.

That is why Wiccan apologetics is not only useful—it is necessary.

Even now, in the twenty-first century, Wiccans may still find themselves accused of worshipping evil, manipulating unseen forces, or following a path that is somehow "less legitimate" than the world's more dominant religions. These accusations are not just theological errors; they are echoes of a long history of fear and misinformation—echoes that have, at times, turned violent. The persecution of wise women and "cunning men" in past centuries may seem like ancient history, but its shadow still lingers in the assumptions and attitudes some people carry today.

Beyond the dramatic misconceptions lie subtler but no less damaging ones: the idea that Wicca is "just a phase," a trend, or a theatrical hobby. Or that it's an individualistic, do-what-you-want mishmash with no moral center. Such portrayals not only disrespect the depth and seriousness of Wiccan spiritual life, they obscure its rich ethical framework, its reverence for balance, and its commitment to personal responsibility.

Wiccan apologetics offers an antidote to all this—not with fury, but with facts. Not by retreating into silence, but by stepping forward with poise. It is an opportunity to correct the record, to represent the path with authenticity, and to affirm for ourselves and others that Wicca is a tradition of depth, beauty, and integrity.

And perhaps most importantly, Wiccan apologetics allows Wiccans to *own* their own stories. For too long, others have spoken *about* Wicca without ever listening to Wiccans. This chapter, and the work it invites us to do, reclaims the narrative. It says: Wiccans will speak for ourselves, in our own words, with clarity and care.

In doing so, Wiccans do not seek superiority, nor dominance, nor to convert others to the Wiccan path. Rather, Wiccans seek understanding—and with it, peace. For when people understand what Wicca truly is, the fear fades. The myths fall away. And in that space, real connection can grow.

III. Foundations of Wiccan Belief

At the heart of every religious path lies a set of core truths—a way of seeing the world and living within it. Wicca is no different. While its traditions may vary from coven to coven, or between solitary practitioners, Wicca is built upon foundational beliefs that are consistent in spirit and deeply meaningful to those who walk the path. While we have covered these points in prior chapters, I want to set them out in brief again, before going into specifics on the misconceptions and attacks that Wicca and Wiccans may suffer.

1. The Wiccan Rede and the Ethics of Harm None

The Wiccan Rede—*"An it harm none, do what ye will"*—is often quoted, sometimes misunderstood, and always central. Far from a license for reckless freedom, it is an invitation to mindfulness. It reminds us that we are responsible for our actions, and that our freedom is bounded by the well-being of others and of the world around us. "Harm none" is not a loophole—it is a sacred obligation to live in harmony with all that exists.

This principle echoes through Wiccan ethics, encouraging compassion, restraint, and personal accountability. It asks each practitioner not simply to avoid doing wrong, but to actively consider the ripple effects of their choices. In a world where harm often goes unseen or unacknowledged, this ethical anchor calls us to live with open eyes and open hearts.

2. The Rule of Three and Spiritual Responsibility

Closely linked to the Rede is the Rule of Three: the belief that whatever energy a person puts into the world—positive or negative—returns to them threefold. Though often mistaken for karma or punishment, it is best understood as a spiritual mirror, a teaching that underscores the power of intention and the interconnectedness of all things.

Whether interpreted literally or symbolically, the Rule of Three encourages practitioners to think carefully about what they send out into the world, in word, deed, or magical working. It is not a threat—it is a reminder that we are participants in a sacred web, and what we do resonates beyond ourselves.

3. The Divine as Immanent: God, Goddess, and Sacred Balance

Wicca recognizes the Divine as both immanent and transcendent. The sacred is not distant or removed, but present in nature, in the self, and in the rhythms of the earth. Most Wiccans honor both a Goddess and a God, seen not as rigid gender roles but as archetypal forces—creative, nurturing, wild, wise, ever-shifting, and interwoven.

This divine polarity expresses balance rather than opposition. The Goddess may be seen as Maiden, Mother, and Crone—each phase reflecting a season of life. The God may be honored as the Horned One, the Green Man, or the Sacrificed King, mirroring the cycles of growth and renewal.

Some Wiccans focus primarily on the Goddess; others embrace a broader pantheon, or see deity as symbolic of natural forces. But the common thread is this: the sacred is not "out there." It is *here*, present in soil and star, in breath and heartbeat.

4. Ritual and the Wheel of the Year

Wicca is a religion of rhythm. Ritual plays a central role—not as empty ceremony, but as a way of aligning the self with the cycles of nature and the Divine. Whether in coven circles or solitary rites, rituals honor the turning of the seasons, the waxing and waning of the moon, the milestones of life, and the presence of the sacred in all things.

The Wheel of the Year, with its eight Sabbats, guides practitioners through a spiritual calendar grounded in earth's rhythms. These celebrations—Samhain, Yule, Imbolc, Ostara, Beltane, Litha, Lammas, and Mabon—connect Wiccans to the eternal dance of light and dark, death and rebirth, rest and renewal.

5. Magic as Spiritual Practice

In Wicca, magic is not about control or domination—it is about connection. It is the art of working in harmony with natural energies to bring about change, healing, or clarity. It is an act of reverence, not ego; of intent, not manipulation.

Wiccans see magic as a spiritual tool—one that requires responsibility, respect, and alignment with ethical values. Whether through candle spells, herbal work, divination, or sacred symbols, magic is a way of deepening one's relationship with the unseen threads of existence. It is not supernatural—it is *super-natural*, rooted in the very fabric of the world we inhabit.

Perfect—that's exactly the balance we want in this chapter: reinforcing key principles while reframing them through the lens of understanding and articulation.

Here is the full draft of **Section IV: Addressing Common Misconceptions**:

IV. Addressing Common Misconceptions

Misconceptions about Wicca are not new. They are, unfortunately, part of the landscape Wiccans have always had to navigate—born from cultural misunderstanding, religious intolerance, sensational media, and plain ignorance. One of the most important goals of Wiccan apologetics is not just to defend against these misunderstandings, but to transform them into opportunities for clarity, dialogue, and truth.

What follows are some of the most common misconceptions about Wicca, and ways to address them with both honesty and grace.

1. "Wiccans worship the devil."

This is perhaps the most persistent and harmful myth, especially in communities influenced by Christian or Muslim theology. It is also entirely false. Wiccans do not worship Satan—nor do they even acknowledge Satan as part of their belief system. The concept of the devil is a product of Christian and Muslim cosmology and does not exist within Wiccan theology.

Wiccans honor the Divine in the form of nature-based deities, often represented as a Goddess and a God. The God is sometimes depicted with horns—echoing ancient fertility symbols and nature spirits like Cernunnos or the Green Man. Unfortunately, these horned images have been wrongly equated with the devil. In truth, they represent life, wilderness, and the sacred masculine in balance with the feminine.

2. "Wicca is a made-up religion with no history."

Wicca as a named and organized religious movement is modern—largely emerging in the mid-20th century through the work of figures like Gerald Gardner. But its roots run far deeper. Wicca draws from ancient pre-Christian European traditions, folk magic, seasonal festivals, and reverence for the earth. It also incorporates elements from ceremonial magic, mysticism, and esoteric philosophy.

All religions began *somewhere*. Wicca, though modern in name, is heir to a rich spiritual heritage. Its modern form does not invalidate its authenticity—just as the relative youth of other contemporary spiritual movements does not make them less sincere or meaningful.

3. "Wiccans cast spells to control people."

The idea that Wiccans use magic to manipulate others is both offensive and fundamentally inaccurate. In Wicca, magic is not coercion—it is communion. It is the spiritual art of focusing energy, setting intention, and working in harmony with nature's rhythms to bring about change, healing, insight, or growth.

Ethical Wiccans are bound by principles like the Rede and the Rule of Three. Most would never consider magic that violates another person's will. Spells are often focused inward—on peace, clarity, health, or spiritual transformation—or outward, toward healing, justice, and protection. Magic, in Wicca, is sacred. It is not about power over others; it is about harmony with the world.

4. "Wicca has no moral structure."

This myth often arises from the fact that Wicca has no centralized scripture or governing authority. But, Wiccan ethics are both clear and deeply held. The long version of the Rede is a stronger and clearer base than many religious systems with centralized writings.

The Rede's call to "harm none," the Rule of Three's emphasis on spiritual consequence, and the commitment to balance and respect all speak to a moral framework grounded in personal responsibility. Wiccan ethics are lived, not dictated. They arise from conscious choice, not external command.

5. "Wicca is anti-Christian (or anti-religion)."

Wicca is not a rejection of Christianity—it is a separate path entirely. While some Wiccans may have left other religious traditions due to personal reasons, Wicca does not define itself in opposition to any one faith. It is a religion rooted in reverence for nature, balance, and personal spiritual experience.

Many Wiccans hold respect for people of other faiths and are happy to engage in interfaith dialogue. Wiccan apologetics does not aim to tear down others' beliefs—it aims to explain our own, in hopes of fostering respect and mutual understanding.

6. **"Wicca is just a phase or fantasy."**

Because Wicca encourages personal exploration and symbolic language, it is sometimes dismissed as unserious or juvenile. But this view ignores the devotion, discipline, and spiritual depth of Wiccan practice.

For many practitioners, Wicca is a lifelong spiritual path—a source of meaning, strength, and sacred connection. Like any faith, it has room for seekers and beginners, but its heart is enduring and profound.

Wiccan apologetics begins when we gently but firmly correct these myths. Not with defensiveness, but with clarity. Not to win arguments, but to build bridges. Because behind every misunderstanding is an opportunity to be heard—and behind every question, a door that may open.

V. The Role of Personal Experience in Wicca

Wicca is not a religion of dogma—it is a religion of *doing*, of *being*, of *experiencing*. At its core, Wicca invites the practitioner into direct relationship with the Divine, with nature, with the cycles of life, and with their own inner landscape. While many religious traditions prioritize sacred texts, Wicca places sacred value on lived experience.

For the Wiccan, truth is not handed down from authority—it is discovered in the dance of moonlight, in the stillness of meditation, in the fire of ritual. This is not to say that Wicca lacks structure or teaching—quite the opposite. But it means that Wiccan knowledge is deeply personal, often intuitive, and profoundly embodied.

1. Experience as Sacred Revelation

Wicca teaches that the sacred can be known through experience. To cast a circle, to invoke the elements, to celebrate the turning of the Wheel of the Year—these are not empty gestures. They are doorways to the numinous. Each rite is a conversation between the self and the cosmos, a moment when the veil between the worlds grows thin.

This emphasis on personal revelation makes Wicca both profoundly empowering and difficult to explain to those outside the faith. For how does one convey what it *feels* like when the Goddess is present? Or what it *means* to see the Divine in the budding of spring or the falling of autumn leaves?

Wiccan apologetics, then, must hold space for the ineffable. It must embrace the fact that while not all truths can be proven, they can still be *known*—in the marrow, in the soul, in the hush of the ritual chamber.

2. Subjective Truth Does Not Mean Chaos

Critics sometimes claim that because Wicca does not require adherence to a single holy book or creed, it must therefore lack coherence or seriousness. But this misses the point entirely.

Wicca respects the diversity of spiritual experience because it honors the diversity of nature itself. Just as the forest is made of many trees, Wicca allows for many ways to encounter the sacred. Subjective truth does not mean *anything goes*—it means that truth arises through sincere seeking, reflection, and lived wisdom.

The standards for authenticity in Wicca are not external—they are internal: respect for the sacred, alignment with ethical principles, and integrity in word and deed.

In comparison, there are thousands of sects of Christianity - and at least three major sects of Islam, and they have fought endless, bloody wars with each other both within the two traditions and between the two traditions because they insist on adherence to holy books that they themselves cannot always agree on, even within a given tradition.

3. Inner Work as Outer Practice

Wiccan practice is often outwardly beautiful—candles, incense, robes, ritual tools. But beneath these symbols lies a deeply personal inner journey. The true altar is within. The real spell is the intention. The most powerful ritual may be the one done in silence, under the stars, with no one watching but the Divine.

Wiccan experience is not about spectacle—it is about sincerity. It teaches that transformation begins in the self, and that personal growth is both magical and sacred. In this way, Wicca echoes the mystery traditions of the ancient world: those who come to it must be prepared to change, not just the world, but themselves.

4. The Challenge of Explaining the Mystical

For those unused to mystical or esoteric traditions, Wicca's emphasis on experience can be confusing. How does one explain trance? Or the feeling of energy shifting during a ritual? Or the intuitive bond between a priestess and the lunar cycle?

The answer is: you don't explain *all* of it. Some things must be experienced to be understood. But Wiccan apologetics *can* help prepare the ground. It can demystify the vocabulary, offer analogies, and speak to the universal human hunger for connection, meaning, and beauty.

Experience is not a weakness in a religious path. It is its heart. And in Wicca, that heart beats strong.

VI. Building Bridges: Speaking to the Curious and the Critical

Wiccan apologetics is not merely about correcting misconceptions—it is about fostering understanding. In a world so often divided by difference, the Wiccan practitioner who chooses to speak from a place of clarity and compassion becomes a bridge-builder. And that is sacred work.

Whether speaking to a curious friend, a skeptical relative, or a misinformed critic, the Wiccan voice of reasoned explanation carries power. But that power must be wielded with care. For in apologetics, the *tone* is often as important as the *truth*.

1. Choosing the Path of Calm, Not Combat

There will always be those who challenge or even attack Wicca—some from ignorance, others from fear, and a few from deliberate malice. But not every disagreement requires a battle. Wiccan apologetics is not a sword—it is a staff: a tool of balance, support, and steadiness.

Meeting criticism with anger rarely leads to transformation. But calm, thoughtful conversation—especially when paired with confident knowledge—can be disarming in the best way. Sometimes, the most powerful act of resistance is to respond with peace.

2. Explaining Without Preaching

Wicca is not a proselytizing religion. There are no Wiccan missionaries, no calls to conversion, no door-to-door evangelism. And so, Wiccan apologetics does not seek to *win souls*, but to *open minds*.

The best apologetic stance is one of invitation. Rather than declaring, "This is what *you* should believe," the Wiccan practitioner might say, "This is what I believe, and why it holds meaning for me." This shift from argument to sharing changes the entire dynamic. It centers sincerity over persuasion and allows for dialogue rather than debate.

3. Anticipating the Questions

When someone expresses curiosity about Wicca, it is often because they are encountering it for the first time—or have only seen it through media lenses. Common questions may include:

- "Do you really believe in magic?"

- "Is Wicca a real religion?"

- "Aren't you worried about going to hell?"

- "What do your rituals actually do?"

- "How does Wicca deal with right and wrong?"

A well-prepared Wiccan can meet these questions not as threats, but as opportunities—moments to gently plant seeds of understanding. Not every answer needs to be complex. Sometimes, a simple, "That's a great question. Here's how I understand it…" is enough.

4. Emphasizing Shared Values

One of the most effective tools in apologetics is the ability to *find common ground*. While Wiccan beliefs may differ sharply from those of mainstream religions, they are built upon values that many people hold dear:

- A commitment to peace and non-harm

- Respect for life and the natural world

- Personal responsibility and spiritual growth

- Celebration of seasonal and life cycles

M Community, ritual, and reverence

By highlighting these shared values, the Wiccan practitioner can show that beneath the unfamiliar symbols lies a deeply human spirituality—one rooted in love, not fear; in harmony, not rebellion.

5. Knowing When to Speak—and When to Step Back

Not every conversation will bear fruit. Some people are not ready to listen. Others may wish only to argue. Part of Wiccan wisdom is knowing when to share—and when to protect one's peace. Apologetics is not about forcing the truth into closed ears. It is about lighting a path for those willing to walk it.

And sometimes, the best response to hostility is silence—not the silence of retreat, but the silence of strength.

To speak as a Wiccan in the modern world is, in many ways, an act of bravery. To speak well, with grace and grounded truth, is an act of beauty. Each conversation—whether gentle or difficult—is a chance to show the world what Wicca really is: not a threat, not a fad, but a living tradition of wisdom, reverence, and joy.

VII. Conclusion: Wisdom as the Highest Defense

To walk the Wiccan path is to move through the world with both reverence and resilience. It is to recognize the sacred in the soil, the storm, the stars—and also in the questions, the challenges, and the conversations that arise when we share that path with others.

Wiccan apologetics is not about winning arguments or proving superiority. It is not about shouting louder or outwitting critics. It is about something older, quieter, and far more powerful: *wisdom*.

Wisdom listens before it speaks. It chooses its words with care. It knows that timing matters—that sometimes a seed of understanding needs years to bloom. Wisdom recognizes that not everyone who asks a question is ready for an answer. And it also knows that sometimes, the simple act of speaking one's truth with clarity and dignity can change everything.

Wiccans carry their truth not on banners, but in their very bones. Their defense is not found in scripture, but in the steadiness of their presence. Their strength lies not in how loudly they speak, but in how clearly they *live* their values.

When they choose to engage in apologetics, they are not just defending a tradition—they are embodying it. They become its face, its voice, its hands. They show that Wicca is not shadowy or fringe, but luminous and alive. That it is not a retreat from reason, but a reunion with the sacred.

In a world where misunderstanding is easy and fear is loud, wisdom becomes the greatest ally. It does not falter in the face of scrutiny. It does not lash out when challenged. It stands, calm and rooted, like the oak in the storm.

And so we close this chapter with a simple truth: when people speak as Wiccans—with honesty, with insight, with kindness—they do more than correct misconceptions. They offer a glimpse of something beautiful, whole, and quietly radiant.

They offer the world the gift of *understanding*—and in that, they offer peace.

Appendices - A

Sacred Songs and Epic Psalms to the divine feminine, from ancient sources

The Courtship of Inanna and Dumuzi

(D. Wolkenstein, *Inanna* [Harper & Row 1983], 30-49)

(1)

The brother spoke to his younger sister.

The Sun God, Utu, spoke to Inanna, saying:

—*Young Lady, the flax in its fullness is lovely.*

Inanna, the grain is glistening in the furrow.

I will hoe it for you. I will bring it to you.

A piece of linen, big or small, is always needed.

Inanna, I will bring it to you.

—*Brother, after you've brought me the flax,*

Who will comb it for me?

—*Sister, I will bring it to you combed.*

—*Utu, after you've brought it to me combed,*

Who will spin it for me?

—*Inanna, I will bring it to you spun.*

—*Brother, after you've brought the flax to be spun,*

Who will braid it for me?

—*Sister, I will bring it to you braided.*

—*Utu, after you've brought it to me braided,*

Who will weave it for me?

—*Sister, I will bring it to you woven.*

—*Utu, after you've brought it to me woven,*

Who will bleach it for me?

—*Inanna, I will bring it to you bleached.*

—*Brother, after you've brought my bridal sheet to me,*

Who will go to bed with me?

Utu, who will go to bed with me?

—*Sister, your bridegroom will go to bed with you.*

He who was born from a fertile womb,

He who was conceived on the sacred marriage throne,

Dumuzi, the shepherd! He will go to bed with you.

(2)

Inanna spoke:

—*No, brother!*

The man of my heart works the hoe.

The farmer! He is the man of my heart!

He gathers the grain into great heaps.

He brings the grain regularly into my storehouses.

Utu spoke:

—Sister, marry the shepherd.

Why are you unwilling?

His cream is good; his milk is good.

Whatever he touches shines brightly.

Inanna, marry Dumuzi.

You who adorn yourself with the agate necklace of fertility,

Why are you unwilling?

Dumuzi will share his rich cream with you.

You who are meant to be the king's protector,

Why are you unwilling?

Inanna spoke:

—The shepherd? I will not marry the shepherd!

His clothes are coarse; his wool is rough.

I will marry the farmer.

The farmer grows flax for my clothes,

The farmer grows barley for my table.

Dumuzi spoke:

—Why do you speak about the farmer?

Why do you speak about him?

If he gives you black flour,

I will give you black wool.

If he gives you white flour,

I will give you white wool.

If he gives you beer,

I will give you sweet milk.

If he gives you bread,

I will give you honey cheese.

I will give the farmer my leftover cream.

I will give the farmer my leftover milk.

Why do you speak about the farmer?

What does he have more than I do?

Inanna spoke:

—Shepherd, without my mother, Ningal, you'd be driven away,

without my grandmother, Ningikuga, you'd be driven into the steeps,

without my father, Nanna, you'd have no roof,

without my brother Utu—

Dumuzi spoke:

—Inanna, do not start a quarrel.

My father, Enki, is as good as your father, Nanna.

My mother, Sirtur, is as good as your mother, Ningal.

My sister, Geshtinanna, is as good as yours.

Queen of the palace, let us talk it over.

The word they had spoken

Was a word of desire.

From the starting of the quarrel

Came the lovers' desire.

The shepherd went to the royal house with cream.

Dumuzi went to the royal house with milk.

Before the door, he called out:

—*Open the house, My Lady, open the house!*

Inanna ran to Ningal, the mother who bore her.

Ningal counseled her daughter, saying:

—*My child, the young man will be your father.*

My daughter, the young man will be your mother.

He will treat you like a father.

He will care for you like a mother.

Open the house, My Lady, open the house!

(3)

Inanna, at her mother's command,

Bathed and anointed herself with scented oil.

She covered her body with the royal white robe.

She readied her dowry.

She arranged her precious lapis beads around her neck.

She took her seal in her hand.

Dumuzi waited expectantly.

Inanna opened the door for him.

Inside the house she shone before him.

Like the light of the moon.

Dumuzi looked at her joyously.

He pressed his neck close against hers.

He kissed her.

(4)

Inanna spoke:

—What I tell you

Let the singer weave into song.

What I tell you,

Let it flow from ear to mouth,

Let it pass from old to young:

My vulva, the horn,

The Boat of Heaven,

Is full of eagerness like the young moon.

My untilled land lies fallow.

As for me, Inanna,

Who will plow my vulva?

Who will plow my high field?

Who will plow my wet ground?

As for me, the young woman,

Who will plow my vulva?

Who will station the ox there?

Who will plow my vulva?

Dumuzi replied:

—*Great Lady, the king will plow your vulva.*

I, Dumuzi the King, will plow your vulva.

Inanna:

—*Then plow my vulva, man of my heart!*

Plow my vulva!

At the king's lap stood the rising cedar.

Plants grew high by their side.

Grains grew high by their side.

Gardens flourished luxuriantly.

(5)

Inanna sang:

—*He has sprouted; he has burgeoned;*

He is lettuce planted by the water.

He is the one my womb loves best.

My well-stocked garden of the plain,

My barley growing high in its furrow,

My apple tree which bears fruit up to its crown,

He is lettuce planted by the water.

My honey-man, my honey-man sweetens me always.

My lord, the honey-man of the gods,

He is the one my womb loves best.

His hand is honey, his foot is honey,

He sweetens me always.

My eager impetuous caresser of the navel,

My caresser of the soft thighs,

He is the one my womb loves best.

He is lettuce planted by the water.

(6)

Dumuzi sang:

—*O Lady, your breast is your field.*

Inanna, your breast is your field.

Your broad field pours out the plants.

Your broad field pours out grain.

Water flows from on high for your servant.

Bread flows from on high for your servant.

Pour it out for me, Inanna.

I will drink all you offer.

(7)

Inanna sang:

—Make your milk sweet and thick, my bridegroom.

My shepherd, I will drink your fresh milk.

Wild bull Dumuzi, make your milk sweet and thick.

I will drink your fresh milk.

Let the milk of the goat flow in my sheepfold.

Fill my holy churn with honey cheese.

Lord Dumuzi, I will drink your fresh milk.

My husband, I will guard my sheepfold for you.

I will watch over your house of life, the storehouse,

The shining quivering place which delights Sumer—

The house which decides the fates of the land,

The house which gives the breath of life to the people.

I, the queen of the palace, will watch over your house.

Dumuzi spoke:

—My sister, I would go with you to my garden.

Inanna, I would go with you to my garden.

I would go with you to my orchard.

I would go with you to my apple tree.

There I would plant the sweet, honey-covered seed.

Inanna spoke:

—He brought me into his garden.

My brother, Dumuzi, brought me into his garden.

I strolled with him among the standing trees,

I stood with him among the fallen trees,

By the apple tree I knelt as is proper.

Before my brother coming in song,

Who rose to me out of poplar leaves,

Who came to me in the midday heat,

Before my lord, Dumuzi,

I poured out plants from my womb.

I placed plants before him,

I poured out plants before him.

I placed grain before him,

I poured out grain before him,

I poured out grain before my womb.

Inanna sang:

—Last night as I, the queen, was shining bright,

Last night as I, the Queen of Heaven, was shining bright,

As I was shining bright and dancing,

Singing praises at the coming of the night—

He met me—he met me!

My lord Dumuzi met me.

He pushed his hand to my hand.

He pressed his neck close against mine.

My high priest is ready for the holy loins.

My lord Dumuzi is ready for the holy loins.

The plants and herbs in his field are ripe.

O Dumuzi! Your fullness is my delight!

(8)

She called for it, she called for it, she called for the bed!

She called for the bed that rejoices the heart.

She called for the bed that sweetens the loins.

She called for the bed of kingship.

She called for the bed of queenship.

Inanna called for the bed:

—*Let the bed that rejoices the heart be prepared!*

Let the bed that sweetens the loins be prepared!

Let the bed of kingship be prepared!

Let the bed of queenship be prepared!

Let the royal bed be prepared!

Inanna spread the bridal sheet across the bed.

She called to the king:

—*The bed is ready!*

She called to her bridegroom:

—*The bed is waiting!*

He put his hand in her hand.

He put his hand to her heart.

Sweet is the sleep of the hand-to-hand.

Sweeter still is the sleep of heart-to-heart.

(9)

Inanna spoke:

—*I bathed for the wild bull,*

I bathed for the shepherd Dumuzi,

I perfumed my sides with ointment,

I coated my mouth with sweet-smelling amber,

I painted my eyes with kohl.

He shaped my loins with his fair hands.

The shepherd Dumuzi filled my lap with cream and milk,

He stroked my pubic hair,

He watered my womb.

He laid his hands on my holy vulva,

He smoothed my black boat with cream,

He quickened my narrow boat with milk,

He creased me on the bed.

Now I will caress my high priest on the bed,

I will caress the faithful shepherd Dumuzi,

I will caress his loins, the shepherdship of the land,

I will decree a sweet fate for him.

The Queen of Heaven,

The heroic woman, greater than her mother,

Who was presented the divine powers by Enki,

Inanna, the First Daughter of the Moon,

Decreed the fate of Dumuzi:

—In battle I am you leader,

In combat I am your armor-bearer

In the assembly I am your advocate,

On the campaign I am your inspiration.

You, the chosen shepherd of the holy shrine,

You, the king, the faithful provider of Uruk,

You, the light of An's great shrine,

In all ways you are fit:

To hold you head high on the loft dais,

To sit on the lapis lazuli throne,

To cover you head with the holy crown,

To wear long clothes on your body,

To bind yourself with the garments of kingship,

To carry the mace and sword,

To guide straight the long bow and arrow,

To fasten the throw-stick and sling at your side,

To race on the road with the holy scepter in your hand,

And the holy sandals on your feet,

To prance on the holy breast like a lapis lazuli calf.

You, the sprinter, the chosen shepherd,

In all ways you are fit.

May your heart enjoy long days.

That which An has determined for you—may it not be altered.

That which Enlil has granted—may it not be changed.

You are the favorite of Ningal.

Inanna holds you dear.

Ninshubur, the faithful servant of the holy shrine of Uruk,

Led Dumuzi to the sweet thighs of Inanna and spoke:

—My queen, here is the choice of your heart,

the king, your beloved bridegroom.

May he spend long days in the sweetness of your holy loins.

Give him a favorable and glorious reign.

Grant him the king's throne, firm in its foundations.

Grant him the shepherd's staff of judgment.

Grant him the enduring crown with the radiant and noble diadem.

From where the sun rises to where the sun sets,

From north to south,

From the Upper Sea to the Lower Sea,

From the land of the huluppu-tree to the land of the cedar,

Let his shepherd's staff protect all of Sumer and Akkad.

As the farmer, let him make the fields fertile,

As the shepherd, let him make the sheepfolds multiply,

Under his reign let there be vegetation,

Under his reign let there be rich grain.

In the marshland may the fish and birds chatter,

In the canebrake may the young and old reeds grow high,

In the steppe may the deer and wild goats multiply,

In the orchards may there be honey and wine,

In the grasslands may the lettuce and cress grow high,

In the palace may there be long life.

May there be floodwater in the Tigris and Euphrates,

May the plants grow high on their banks and fill the meadows,

May the Lady of Vegetation pile the grain in heaps and mounds.

O my Queen of Heaven and Earth,

Queen of all the universe,

May he enjoy long days in the sweetness of your holy loins.

The king went with lifted head to the holy loin.

He went with lifted head to the loins of Inanna.

He went to the queen with lifted head.

He opened wide his arms to the holy priestess of heaven.

Inanna spoke:

—*My beloved, the delight of my eyes, met me.*

We rejoiced together.

He took his pleasure of me.

He brought me into his house.

He laid me down on the fragrant honey-bed.

My sweet love, lying by my heart,

Tongue-playing, one by one,

My fair Dumuzi did so fifty times.

Now, my sweet love is sated.

Now he says:

"Set me free, my sister, set me free.

You will be a little daughter to my father.

Come, my beloved sister, I would go to the palace.

Set me free..."

Inanna spoke:

—*My brother-brearer, your allure was sweet.*

My blossom-bearer in the apple orchard,

My bearer of fruit in the apple orchard,

Dumuzi-abzu, your allure was sweet.

My fearless one,

My holy statue,

My statue outfitted with sword and lapis lazuli diadem,

How sweet was your allure...

Descent of the Goddess Ishtar Into the Lower World

(The Civilization of Babylonia and Assyria, M. Jastrow, 1915)

To the land of no return, the land of darkness,

Ishtar, the daughter of Sin directed her thought,

Directed her thought, Ishtar, the daughter of Sin,

To the house of shadows, the dwelling, of Irkalla,

To the house without exit for him who enters therein,

To the road, whence there is no turning,

To the house without light for him who enters therein,

The place where dust is their nourishment, clay their food.'

They have no light, in darkness they dwell.

Clothed like birds, with wings as garments,

Over door and bolt, dust has gathered.

Ishtar on arriving at the gate of the land of no return,

To the gatekeeper thus addressed herself:

"Gatekeeper, ho, open thy gate!

Open thy gate that I may enter!

If thou openest not the gate to let me enter,

I will break the door, I will wrench the lock,

I will smash the door-posts, I will force the doors.

I will bring up the dead to eat the living.

And the dead will outnumber the living."

The gatekeeper opened his mouth and spoke,

Spoke to the lady Ishtar:

"Desist, O lady, do not destroy it.

I will go and announce thy name to my queen Ereshkigal."

The gatekeeper entered and spoke to Ereshkigal:

"Ho! here is thy sister, Ishtar ...

Hostility of the great powers ...

When Ereshkigal heard this,

As when one hews down a tamarisk she trembled,

As when one cuts a reed, she shook:

"What has moved her heart [seat of the intellect] what has stirred her liver [seat of the emotions]?

Ho there, does this one wish to dwell with me?

To eat clay as food, to drink dust as wine?

I weep for the men who have left their wives.

I weep for the wives torn from the embrace of their husbands;

For the little ones cut off before their time.

Go, gatekeeper, open thy gate for her,

Deal with her according to the ancient decree."

The gatekeeper went and opened his gate to her:

Enter, O lady, let Cuthah greet thee.

Let the palace of the land of no return rejoice at thy presence!

He bade her enter the first gate, which he opened wide, and took the large crown off her head:

"Why, O gatekeeper, dost thou remove the large crown off my head?"

"Enter, O lady, such are the decrees of Ereshkigal."

The second gate he bade her enter, opening it wide, and removed her earrings:

"Why, O gatekeeper, dost thou remove my earrings?"

"Enter, O lady, for such are the decrees of Ereshkigal."

The third gate he bade her enter, opened it wide, and removed her necklace:

"Why, O gatekeeper, dost thou remove my necklace?"

"Enter, O lady, for such are the decrees of Ereshkigal."

The fourth gate he bade her enter, opened it wide, and removed the ornaments of her breast:

"Why, O gatekeeper, dost thou remove the ornaments of my breast?"

"Enter, O lady, for such are the decrees of Ereshkigal."

The fifth gate he bade her enter, opened it wide, and removed the girdle of her body studded with birthstones.

"Why, O gatekeeper, dost thou remove the girdle of my body, studded with birth-stones?"

"Enter, O lady, for such are the decrees of Ereshkigal."

The sixth gate, he bade her enter, opened it wide, and removed the spangles off her hands and feet.

"Why, O gatekeeper, dost thou remove the spangles off my hands and feet?"

"Enter, O lady, for thus are the decrees of Ereiihkigal."

The seventh gate he bade her enter, opened it wide, and removed her loin-cloth.

"Why, O gatekeeper, dost thou remove my loin-cloth?"

"Enter, O lady, for such are the decrees of Ereshkigal."

Now when Ishtar had gone down into the land of no return,

Ereshkigal saw her and was angered at her presence.

Ishtar, without reflection, threw herself at her [in a rage].

Ereshkigal opened her mouth and spoke,

To Namtar, her messenger, she addressed herself:

"Go Namtar, imprison her in my palace.

Send against her sixty disease, to punish Ishtar.

Eye-disease against her eyes,

Disease of the side against her side,

Foot-disease against her foot,

Heart-disease against her heart,

Head-disease against her head,

Against her whole being, against her entire body."

After the lady Ishtar had gone down into the land of no return,

The bull did not mount the cow, the ass approached not the she-ass,

To the maid in the street, no man drew near

The man slept in his apartment,

The maid slept by herself.

[The second half of the poem, the reverse of the tablet, continues is follows:]

The countenance of Papsukal, the messenger of the great gods, fell, his face was troubled.

In mourning garb he was clothed, in soiled garments clad.

Shamash [the sun-god] went to Sin [the moon-god], his father, weeping,

In the presence of Ea, the King, he went with flowing tears.

"Ishtar has descended into the earth and has not come up. The bull does not mount the cow, the ass does not approach the she-ass.

The man does not approach the maid in the street,

The man sleeps in his apartment,

The maid sleeps by herself."

Ea, in the wisdom of his heart, formed a being,

He formed Asu-shu-namir the eunuch.

Go, Asu-shu-namir, to the land of no return direct thy face!

The seven gates of the land without return be opened before thee,

May Eresbkigal at sight of thee rejoice!

After her heart has been assuaged, her liver quieted,

Invoke against her the name of the great gods,

Raise thy head direct thy attention to the khalziku skin.

"Come, lady, let them give me the khalziku skin, that I may drink water out of it."

When Ereshkigal heard this, she struck her side, bit her finger,

Thou hast expressed a wish that can not be granted.

Go, Asu-shu-iaamir, I curse thee with a great curse,

The sweepings of the gutters of the city be thy food,

The drains of the city be thy drink,

The shadow of the wall be thy abode,

The thresholds be thy dwelling-place;

Drunkard and sot strike thy cheek!"

Ereshkigal opened her mouth and spoke,

To Namtar, her messenger, she addressed herself.

"Go, Namtar, knock at the strong palace,

Strike the threshold of precious stones,

Bring out the Anunnaki, seat them on golden thrones.

Sprinkle Ishtar with the waters of life and take her out of my presence.

Namtar went, knocked at the strong palace,

Tapped on the threshold of precious stones.

He brought out the Anunnaki and placed them on golden thrones,

He sprinkled Ishtar with the waters of life and took hold of her.

Through the first gate he led her out and returned to her her loin-cloth.

Through the second gate he led her out and returned to her the spangles of her hands and feet

Through the third gate he led her out and returned to her the girdle of her body, studded with birth-stones.

Through the fourth gate he led her out and returned to her the ornaments of her breast.

Through the fifth gate he led her out and returned to her her necklace.

Through the sixth gate he led her out and returned her earrings.

Through the seventh gate he led her out and returned to her the large crown for her head.

[The following lines are in the form of an address -apparently to some one who has sought release for a dear one from the portals of the lower world.]

"If she (Ishtar) will not grant thee her release,

To Tammuz, the lover of her youth,

Pour out pure waters, pour out fine oil;

With a festival garment deck him that he may play on the flute of lapis lazuli,

That the votaries may cheer his liver. [his spirit]

Belili [sister of Tammuz] had gathered the treasure,

With precious stones filled her bosom.

When Belili heard the lament of her brother, she dropped her treasure,

She scattered the precious stones before her,

"Oh, my only brother, do not let me perish!

On the day when Tammuz plays for me on the flute of lapis lazuli, playing it for me with the porphyry ring.

Together with him, play ye for me, ye weepers and lamenting women!

That the dead may rise up and inhale the incense."

Appendix B –

A Couple of More Modern Songs to Celebrate the Lord and Lady

For Yule – GODS REST YE MERRY PAGAN FOLK

(to the tune of 'God Rest Ye Merry Gentlemen' with lyrics by Zemira Rowan)

Gods rest ye merry pagan folk, let nothing you dismay

Remember that the Sun returns upon this Solstice Day!

The growing dark is ended now and Spring is on its way

CHORUS:

O, tidings of comfort and joy! Comfort and joy!

O, tidings of comfort and joy!

The Winter's worst still lies ahead, fierce tempest, snow and rain!

Beneath the blanket on the ground the spark of life remains!

The Sun's warm rays caress the seeds to raise Life's songs again!

(CHORUS)

Within the blessed apple lies the promise of the Queen!

For from this pentacle shall rise the orchards fresh and green.

The Earth shall blossom once again, the air be sweet and clean!

THE HOLLY AND THE IVY (Pagan version)

The holly and the ivy

When they are both full grown,

Of all the trees that are in the wood

The holly bears the crown.

CHORUS

The rising of the Sun

And the running of the deer,

The twining of the ivy and the

Crying of the bright new year.

The holly and the ivy

And the lying of the Earth,

The yielding of the blessed womb and

The giving of the birth.

(Chorus)

The holly and the ivy

And the glowing of the red,

The blazing of the berries and the

Shining of the golden head.

(Chorus)

The holly and the ivy

And the glowing of the green,

The warming of our blessed Lady

And the flowing of the stream.

(Chorus)

The holly and the ivy,

All the red and all the green,

Great Father Sun and sweet Mother Earth,

Ever blessed King and Queen.

The rising of the Sun

And the running of the deer,

The twining of the ivy and the

Crying of the bright new year.

Appendix C –

A MONTH'S PRIVATE MEDITATIONS. These brief meditations function as a cycle. There are 31 of them to cover a full 31 day month, select out those you least like to ignore if you are using the cycle for a shorter month:

-

Day 1: Awakening the Self

> M **Visualization**: Imagine yourself standing barefoot in a meadow at sunrise. With every breath, golden light fills your chest, waking the spirit within.
>
> M **Goal**: Begins this cycle of meditations by opening your awareness. Today, notice your presence in every action.

-

Day 2: Rooted Strength

> M **Visualization**: See your feet growing roots into the Earth, anchoring you as wind moves through your branches like a great tree.
>
> M **Goal**: Focus on grounding. Let strength come not from resistance, but from rooted stillness.

-

Day 3: Flame of Intention

> M **Visualization**: A single candle burns before you. See yourself gently cupping the flame, feeding it your focused will without extinguishing it.

Goal: Choose one clear intention to guide your day. Feed it with steady focus.

Day 4: Waters of Emotion

Visualization: You kneel by a still pool. Drop a single leaf onto the surface. Watch the ripples move outward and return to stillness.

Goal: Recognize your emotional state. Let it move, flow, and settle—without judgment.

Day 5: Voice of the Wind

Visualization: The wind circles you, whispering words in forgotten tongues. You need not understand, only listen.

Goal: Practice listening—deeply. Let silence speak. Let others speak. Hear the unseen.

Day 6: The Mirror Within

Visualization: Picture a still, obsidian mirror. As you gaze into it, your reflection begins to shift—not into someone else, but into your truest self.

Goal: Reflect honestly today. What masks do you wear? What part of you longs to be seen?

Day 7: Sacred Fire

M **Visualization**: You stand before a ritual fire, its flames dancing with color. One by one, you toss in words you no longer need—fear, doubt, shame.

M **Goal**: Let go. Release a thought, habit, or emotion that no longer serves you. Let it burn cleanly.

Day 8: Path of the Moon

M **Visualization**: You walk a spiral path under a waxing moon. Each step glows with lunar light, leading you inward toward mystery and magic.

M **Goal**: Tune in to subtle energy today. Observe the moon's phase and reflect on what is growing within your spirit.

Day 9: The Whispering Grove

M **Visualization**: Trees surround you—ash, oak, willow. As you sit at the grove's center, the rustling of leaves becomes language. You are not alone.

M **Goal**: Connect with nature. Go outside, even briefly, and greet the green world with reverence and attention.

Day 10: Circle of Protection

M **Visualization**: Envision a sphere of shimmering light around you, pulsing with warmth and safety. Nothing enters without your welcome.

> M **Goal**: Set energetic boundaries today. Protect your time, your space, and your spirit with loving firmness.

Day 11: The Cauldron of Change

> M **Visualization**: A great iron cauldron bubbles at the center of a moonlit clearing. You stir it slowly, watching fears dissolve into steam.

> M **Goal**: Embrace transformation today. Let discomfort be the sign that something new is forming.

Day 12: Threads of Connection

> M **Visualization**: Silver threads extend from your heart, weaving outward—toward loved ones, ancestors, the land, the stars.

> M **Goal**: Acknowledge your place in the great web of life. Reach out to someone, or offer gratitude to those unseen.

Day 13: Light Between the Worlds

> M **Visualization**: You hold a lantern at twilight, walking a misty path. The veil is thin, and soft voices greet you from beyond.

> M **Goal**: Honor the unseen today—spirits, ancestors, guides. Listen gently for signs or synchronicities.

Day 14: Labyrinth of the Self

M **Visualization**: You walk a stone labyrinth with one question in your heart. At the center, you sit and hear the answer echo in your bones.

M **Goal**: Choose one persistent inner question. Sit with it in meditation. The answer may be silence—and that is enough.

Day 15: The Breath of the Earth

M **Visualization**: You lie on the forest floor, your breath rising and falling in rhythm with the soil, the roots, the heartbeat of the Earth.

M **Goal**: Practice conscious breathing today. Let each breath be an offering and a returning.

Day 16: Crown of Stars

M **Visualization**: Above you, a constellation slowly forms—a circlet of stars that settles gently on your brow, filling your thoughts with calm clarity.

M **Goal**: Focus your mind. Today is for clear vision and inspired thought. Wear your wisdom with quiet pride.

Day 17: The Sacred Flame Within

M **Visualization**: Deep within your chest, a tiny flame flickers. You cup your hands around it—not to hide it, but to tend it lovingly.

> M **Goal**: Nourish your inner fire today. Do one thing that brings you joy, strength, or creative spark.

Day 18: Tides of Letting Go

> M **Visualization**: The ocean tide flows over your feet, pulling gently at all that you're ready to release. You let it go, like seafoam.

> M **Goal**: Surrender. Even for a moment, allow something you've been clinging to to drift away. Lighten your soul.

Day 19: Voice of the Ancients

> M **Visualization**: In a circle of standing stones, voices rise in song. They are old—older than words—but you recognize the melody in your bones.

> M **Goal**: Connect with the ancestors today. Light a candle or speak a name aloud. Let memory be a form of magic.

Day 20: The Seed Beneath Snow

> M **Visualization**: You see a single seed lying deep under frozen ground. Though unseen, it is alive—full of silent, patient power.

> M **Goal**: Trust in what is not yet visible. Honor your process, even if no results show yet. Growth is happening underground.

Day 21: The Shadow's Gift

M **Visualization**: In a cave lit only by your own breath, a shadow figure appears—part of you, yet long forgotten. It reaches out not in fear, but in offering.

M **Goal**: Today, honor something within you that you've been avoiding. Even our shadow selves carry wisdom and protection.

Day 22: Chalice of Compassion

M **Visualization**: You hold a silver chalice overflowing with cool, glowing water. You drink deeply, then offer the cup to the world around you.

M **Goal**: Practice compassion today—for others, and for yourself. Offer kindness without expecting a return.

Day 23: Threads of Fate

M **Visualization**: Three women sit at a loom, weaving strands of gold, black, and crimson. As you approach, they hand you a single thread.

M **Goal**: Consider your role in your own destiny. What choices are in your hands today? Act with intention.

Day 24: Dance of the Elements

M **Visualization**: You stand at the crossroads, and one by one the Elements approach—flame, wind, wave, stone. You greet each with a gesture, and then dance with them.

> **M Goal**: Let your body connect today. Move, stretch, sway. Feel the Elements within your own bones and breath.

Day 25: The Still Center

> **M Visualization**: The world spins around you, fast and loud—but you sit cross-legged at the center of a stone circle, utterly still, untouched by the storm.
>
> **M Goal**: Practice quiet today. Even for five minutes, find a moment where you are unmoved by the outer world.

Day 26: The Wandering Star

> **M Visualization**: A lone star drifts across the sky—not part of any constellation, but glowing with purpose. You walk beneath it, trusting its quiet pull.
>
> **M Goal**: Trust your personal path today, even if it diverges from others. The way of the Witch is often solitary—but never without meaning.

Day 27: Cloak of the Crone

> **M Visualization**: A dark figure wraps you in a cloak woven of night skies, owl feathers, and silence. You feel safe, ancient, and wise beyond time.
>
> **M Goal**: Embrace your inner elder today. Make one choice not for speed or gain, but for wisdom.

Day 28: The Flame You Carry

M **Visualization**: In your hands you hold a small, flickering flame passed from an unseen figure. Behind you, others wait. You step forward and pass the flame.

M **Goal**: Be a light-bearer today. Teach something. Encourage someone. Be a link in the lineage of spirit.

Day 29: The Serpent's Coil

M **Visualization**: A great serpent curls around you—not threatening, but coiled in protective spirals. You breathe in its stillness, its ancient knowing.

M **Goal**: Hold your power quietly today. You do not need to prove anything. Be strong in your stillness.

Day 30: Gathering the Threads

M **Visualization**: You sit at a loom, all the threads from your past month flowing toward you. One by one, you weave them into a single, radiant tapestry.

M **Goal**: Reflect today. What has shifted in you over this moon-cycle? What do you now carry that you didn't before?

Day 31: A New Flame

M **Visualization**: You strike flint to stone. A new flame sparks into life. You lift it high—and suddenly, you're not alone. Dozens of others lift their flames with you.

M **Goal**: Begin again. The path does not end—it turns. Carry the work of this month into the next. Light leads on.

Appendix D –

OTHER DEVOTIONAL PRACTICES

Morning Devotions

Purpose: To begin your day in alignment with Spirit and intention.

Suggested Practices:

1. **Greeting the Elements**

Face each direction, offering a word or gesture of respect:

" *East (Air):* "Blessed be the winds that carry thought and clarity."

" *South (Fire):* "Blessed be the flames of passion and will."

" *West (Water):* "Blessed be the waters of feeling and flow."

" *North (Earth):* "Blessed be the stones that ground and sustain."

2. **Light a Candle or Incense**

Choose a scent or color aligned with your intention for the day. As you light it, say:

"I awaken to this day in wisdom, strength, and grace."

3. **Daily Affirmation**

Speak a truth you wish to embody:

"I walk in balance."

"I speak with honesty."

"I honor the Divine in all things."

Evening Devotions

Purpose: To reflect, release, and rest in sacred awareness.

Suggested Practices:

1. **Extinguish the Flame**
   If you lit a morning candle, gently extinguish it while saying:
   "Day is done. Let peace descend. I give thanks."
2. **Gratitude Offering**
   Speak aloud or write down 3 things you are grateful for. Even on difficult days, seek out a moment of beauty, connection, or strength.
3. **Cleansing Breath**
   Take three deep breaths. On the inhale, draw in calm. On the exhale, release the day.
4. **Simple Prayer or Invocation**
   Optional example:
   *"Lady of the Moon, Lord of the Flame,
   I lay down this day in your names.
   Keep me in peace and wisdom's light.
   I rest beneath your stars tonight."*

Weekly Practices for Deeper Connection

Choose one or two to build into your weekly rhythm:

M **Cleanse and tend your altar**

M Offer fresh water or flowers to your deities

M Walk barefoot outdoors with intention

M Write in your spiritual journal or Book of Shadows

☾ Observe the moon's phase and align your energy accordingly

☾ Honor your ancestors with a candle or spoken remembrance

Creating Your Own Daily Practice

These devotions are a starting point, not a prescription. Your path is your own. Begin simply, and build slowly. You might choose just one practice each morning and one each night. Over time, what begins as habit becomes holy.

Remember: every breath can be sacred. Every moment a chance to remember who you are, and why you walk this path.

Appendix E –

A HANDFUL OF SPELLS AND CHARMS FOR EVERYDAY LIFE

Magic in Wicca is the equivalent of prayer in other faiths and is not about commanding the universe, but entering into a respectful relationship with its rhythms. The spells below are meant to be accessible, gentle, and effective—built on clarity of purpose, ethical awareness, and the practitioner's own energy.

Each spell includes:

- Purpose

- Suggested Tools (if any)

- Timing (moon phase or day, if helpful)

- Steps

- Optional Words of Power or charm lines

1. Protection Door Charm

Purpose: To safeguard the home energetically

Tools: A small sachet or pouch, pinch of salt, dried rosemary, and a protective stone (e.g., obsidian or hematite)

Timing: Waning moon or Saturday

Steps:

- - Fill the pouch with salt and rosemary.

- - Add the stone and breathe over it three times.

- - Hang the charm on or near your front door.

Words of Power:

By root and stone, leaf and sea,

Safe this space shall always be.

2. Candle for Clarity

Purpose: To clear the mind and enhance decision-making

Tools: White or pale blue candle

Timing: Waxing moon or Wednesday

Steps:

- - Sit in a quiet place and light the candle.

- - Gaze into the flame and focus on your question or confusion.

- - Breathe deeply and imagine fog lifting from your mind.

Words of Power:

Clear be my thoughts, like morning dew—

Truth arise, fresh and new.

3. Knot Spell for Confidence

Purpose: To summon courage before a challenge

Tools: A short length of red or gold string or yarn

Timing: Morning, or the waxing moon

Steps:

- - Hold the string and visualize strength flowing into you.

- - Tie three knots while repeating an affirmation.

- - Keep the knotted string in a pocket or pouch during the day.

Words of Power:

With this knot I claim my fire.

I walk in strength, I rise, I rise.

4. Herbal Peace Jar

Purpose: To bring harmony to a household or working space

Tools: Small jar, chamomile, lavender, rose petals, paper and pen

Timing: Full moon or Friday

Steps:

- Add herbs to jar with calm breath and intention.
- Write the word peace and fold the paper three times, adding it to the jar.
- Seal the jar and place in a central or quiet spot.

Words of Power:

By leaf and bloom and moonlit art,

Let peace now dwell in every heart.

5. Releasing Spell

Purpose: To let go of an emotion, habit, or situation

Tools: Paper, pen, fire-safe bowl, black or dark blue candle

Timing: Waning moon

Steps:

- Write what you wish to release on the paper.
- Light the candle and sit in reflection.
- Burn the paper in the bowl, visualizing the release fully.

Words of Power:

I thank you, I release you.

Go in peace, and trouble me no more.

6. Full Moon Blessing Bowl

Purpose: To draw blessings, energy, or inspiration into your life

Tools: A small glass or ceramic bowl of water, moonlight

Timing: Full Moon

Steps:

- - Place the bowl under moonlight (outside or on a windowsill).

- - As the moonlight touches the water, say aloud or whisper your blessing or request.

- - In the morning, use the moon-blessed water to anoint your forehead, hands, or altar.

Words of Power:

Moon above, so wise and bright,

Bless this water with your light.

7. Coin of Prosperity

Purpose: To invite abundance or prosperity into your life (ethically and without greed)

Tools: A shiny coin, green cloth, cinnamon or basil, and a small pouch

Timing: Thursday or waxing moon

Steps:

- - Wrap the coin in the cloth with a pinch of herbs.

- - Hold it between your hands and speak your intention aloud.

- Keep it on your altar, in your wallet, or near your front door.

Words of Power:

By effort fair and heart so clear,

Let rightful gain draw gently near.

8. Dreamer's Charm

Purpose: To invite restful sleep and meaningful dreams

Tools: Sachet or fabric square, dried mugwort or lavender, small crystal (like amethyst), string

Timing: Night before rest, preferably waning moon

Steps:

- Add herbs and stone to sachet.

- Whisper your request to the charm and tie it shut.

- Place it under your pillow or beside your bed.

Words of Power:

Dreams come gentle, deep and wise,

Let visions bloom behind my eyes.

9. Focus and Study Spell

Purpose: For clarity during study, reading, writing, or planning

Tools: Yellow candle, sprig of rosemary or peppermint oil

Timing: Morning or waxing moon

Steps:

- Light the candle and inhale the scent of the herb.

- - Sit with spine straight and eyes focused on your task.

- - Rub a dab of oil on your temples or wrists if desired.

Words of Power:

Bright be my mind, steady and sure—

Let knowledge enter and endure.

10. Creativity Awakening Spell

Purpose: To spark artistic or imaginative inspiration

Tools: Orange candle, piece of paper, pen or art tool of choice

Timing: Waxing moon or sunrise

Steps:

- - Light the candle and close your eyes.

- - See yourself creating freely, joyfully, without fear.

- - Write or sketch whatever comes—no judgment, only flow.

Words of Power:

Muse of flame and storm and sea,

Open the gates of creativity.

Appendix F –

A TEMPLATE FOR A BOOK OF SHADOWS (BOOK OF LIGHTS [40])

A *Book of Shadows* (*Book of Lights*) is a personal and sacred record kept by a Wiccan to document their spiritual journey, personal practices, rituals, and insights. It serves as both a journal and a book of practice—a living document that grows and evolves with the practitioner.

Unlike formal religious texts, a Book of Shadows or Book of Lights is uniquely individual. Some are handwritten with ornate illustrations and pressed herbs; others are digital or plain and practical. What matters is the intention behind it: to honor your path, preserve your knowledge, and deepen your relationship with the Divine, nature, and self.

The following is a suggested template for your own personal Book of Shadows or Book of Lights

1. Dedication and Intent

Begin your Book of Shadows with a statement of purpose. Why are you creating this book? What do you hope to learn or honor through it? You may also include a blessing or consecration ritual to dedicate the book as a sacred tool.

2. Personal Beliefs and Ethics

Write out your core spiritual beliefs, the ethical principles that guide your magic, and any personal adaptations or codes you follow. Include notes on the Wiccan Rede, the Rule of Three, or any oaths you may have taken.

3. Deities and Spirit Allies

Include entries for deities you work with, ancestors you honor, or spirit guides and totems. Record your experiences, dreams, messages, and any sacred names or symbols you associate with them.

4. Rituals and Ceremonies

This section is for the rituals you perform: Sabbats, Esbats, personal milestones, dedications, and rites of passage. Note the structure, tools, chants, and results of each one.

5. Spellwork and Charms

Record your spells here. Include purpose, timing, tools, words used, feelings during casting, and the outcome. This becomes your magical reference and a record of your growing skill.

6. Herbal and Crystal Lore

Keep notes on herbs, oils, and crystals you work with—their properties, magical uses, associations, and any personal observations you've made through use.

7. Symbols, Signs, and Dreams

Track recurring symbols, signs from spirit, numerology, astrology notes, or dreams that felt spiritually significant. This section helps you recognize patterns and deepen intuitive wisdom.

8. Moon Phases and Astrology

Note how moon phases and astrological transits affect your energy and magical work. Keep track of Esbats, full moon rituals, and astrological events you've observed or worked with.

9. Daily Reflections or Journaling

Leave space for regular journaling. Write about meditations, devotional practices, challenges, questions, and insights.

10. Index or Table of Contents

Consider numbering your pages and creating a simple index to make your Book of Shadows/ Book of Lights easy to navigate. This is especially useful if your entries are spontaneous or unstructured.

Appendix G –

Creating Personal Spirit Allies or Thoughtform Familiars

In traditional Witchcraft, a *familiar* is understood as a spiritual companion—sometimes a naturally occurring spirit, other times a deliberately created one—who assists the Witch in magical, intuitive, or protective work. While some Wiccans connect with spirit animals, ancestral guides, or deities, others develop **personal spirit allies** or create **thoughtform companions**, often referred to as *constructed familiars* or *servitors*.

This practice requires focused intention, ethical grounding, and spiritual maturity. A thoughtform or familiar should never be treated as a servant or toy—it is a partnership, one formed with responsibility, clarity, and respect.

▪

What Is a Thoughtform or Constructed Familiar?

A **thoughtform** is an energy being created through intention, visualization, and magical will. When carefully formed, it can take on symbolic shape and behavior to aid the practitioner. These entities are not autonomous in the way deities or natural spirits are—but they are responsive, potent, and real within magical consciousness.

A **constructed familiar** is a thoughtform shaped specifically for companionship, magical focus, or subtle protection. Some practitioners imagine them as spirit animals, others as elemental beings, masks, or shadow-selves.

▪

Ethical and Magical Considerations

Before creating a thoughtform or familiar:

- Be clear about your purpose. Is this for protection, focus, companionship, or divination?

- Never use a constructed being to spy on others, manipulate free will, or do harm.

- Respect the being's symbolic nature—it is a reflection of you and your magical energy.

- Plan for release or transformation. No thoughtform should be left unattended indefinitely.

Steps to Create a Thoughtform Familiar

This process can be adapted to suit your tradition, but the structure below provides a solid and ethical framework.

1. Define the Purpose

Write clearly what you intend your familiar to help with. Examples:

- "To help me maintain focus and protection in ritual space."

- "To assist with lunar magic and emotional balance."

- "To serve as a symbolic guardian of my altar."

Keep it simple and respectful.

2. Design the Form

Visualize what the familiar looks like. Ask yourself:

- What form does it take (animal, elemental, abstract shape)?

- What color, size, texture, or symbolic traits does it have?
- What does it represent about your intention?

You may draw or write about it in your Book of Shadows.

3. Choose a Name and Anchor

Give the familiar a name, which becomes the word you speak when calling it.

Then choose a physical **anchor** or **vessel**—a figurine, stone, talisman, or other object where its energy can reside between workings. This item should be treated respectfully and kept safe.

4. Create the Familiar Ritual

This should be done in sacred space. You may:

- Cast a circle
- Call the Elements and your deities if you wish
- Light a candle or incense linked to the familiar's nature
- Speak the purpose aloud
- Visualize its form clearly taking shape in front of you
- Place your hands over the anchor object and breathe energy into it

Speak something like:

"By breath and will, by thought and light,

I call you forth into this rite.

[Name], be born of sacred flame—

I know you, call you, speak your name."

Pause and listen. Sense the energy. When it feels complete, thank and close the rite.

5. Work With the Familiar

When you wish to work with your familiar:

- M Call its name in ritual
- M Hold or place the anchor object on your altar
- M Speak your intention aloud
- M Record results in your magical journal

Over time, the familiar may evolve in form or voice—this is natural and reflective of your own growth.

6. Releasing or Transforming the Familiar

No thoughtform should be left untended indefinitely. When you no longer need the familiar:

- M Thank it for its service
- M Light a candle or incense as offering
- M Speak words of release (e.g., "Return to energy, go in peace.")
- M Bury or cleanse the anchor object, or transform it for new magical purpose

Final Thoughts

Creating a thoughtform familiar is not required in Wiccan practice—but for some, it becomes a deeply personal and empowering magical relationship. If you proceed, do so with intention, respect, and accountability.

The familiar you create will reflect your inner world—so make that world a worthy home.

Appendix H –

CIRCLES[41] – While many Wiccans walk a solitary path, others are drawn to community. Worshiping in a group—often called a circle or coven—can bring support, inspiration, and deeper ritual energy. This appendix offers practical guidance for forming or joining a spiritual group rooted in trust, respect, and shared purpose.

1. Why Work in a Circle?

Group ritual allows for shared energy, co-creation, and collective wisdom. It can be especially powerful during Sabbats, full moons, or rites of passage. For many, a circle becomes both spiritual family and magical laboratory.

2. Types of Groups

Groups may be formal or informal. A coven typically has structure, leadership, and initiatory stages. A study group or ritual circle may be more casual. Define what you're looking for before joining or forming a group.

3. Finding a Group

Seek out groups through local metaphysical shops, open rituals, online communities, or pagan events. Ask questions. Listen. Trust your instincts. A healthy group will welcome honest inquiry and mutual respect.

4. Forming Your Own Circle

If you don't find a group that fits your values, consider starting your own. Begin with one or two trusted friends. Meet regularly, even if informally. Keep things simple. Let your group grow slowly and intentionally.

5. Setting Shared Values

Before diving into ritual, talk openly about group values. Consider: How do we handle disagreement? Is leadership shared? Are rituals closed or open? Clear expectations build strong spiritual bonds.

6. Red Flags and Healthy Boundaries

Avoid groups that use secrecy to control, pressure to conform, or discourage independent thought. Healthy circles respect personal autonomy, consent, and the right to leave at any time without guilt.

7. Creating Ritual Together

Let each member contribute. Roles might rotate—one person leads casting, another calls quarters, another grounds the group. Co-created rituals empower everyone and foster a true sense of shared magic.

8. Sacred Trust

Group work involves vulnerability. Speak kindly. Hold confidences sacred. Support one another through spiritual highs and lows. This trust, when honored, becomes one of the most magical aspects of circle work.

9. Dissolving a Circle

Not all groups are meant to last forever. If your circle no longer serves its purpose, end it with gratitude and grace. Hold a final ritual of thanks. Release each other with blessing.

10. You Are Enough

Whether solitary or in community, your path is valid. Group work is powerful, but not required. If you never find a coven, your magic is no less real, and your spirit no less sacred.

Appendix I –

GLOSSARY OF WICCAN TERMS

This glossary provides definitions for common terms used in Wiccan practice and related Pagan paths. It is intended as a helpful reference for beginners and a refresher for seasoned practitioners. Definitions are concise, clear, and oriented toward practical understanding.

Altar

A sacred space or surface used to place ritual tools, offerings, and symbols of the Divine.

Amulet

An object charged with protective energy, worn or carried to ward off harm or negativity.

Anointing

Applying oil to a person or object as part of a ritual to bless, consecrate, or empower.

Aspecting

The practice of ritually invoking or embodying a deity or spirit during ritual.

Athame

A ritual knife, often black-handled, used to direct energy. Not typically used for physical cutting.

Balefire

A ritual bonfire, often part of Sabbat celebrations, symbolizing purification and transformation.

Banish

To ritually remove unwanted energy, influences, or spirits from a person, object, or place.

Besom

A ritual broom used for symbolic or energetic cleansing of a space before ritual work.

Binding

A spell or ritual performed to restrict or prevent harm, often directed at an individual or influence.

Book of Shadows

A personal magical journal used to record rituals, spells, observations, and spiritual reflections.

Cairn

A pile of stones used as a spiritual marker, often honoring spirits, ancestors, or sacred sites.

Calling the Quarters

Inviting the elemental guardians of North, East, South, and West into ritual space.

Cauldron

A ritual tool symbolizing transformation, often associated with the Goddess or the womb of rebirth.

Chalice

A ritual cup representing the element of Water and often used in the symbolic Great Rite.

Circle

The sacred space cast before ritual, symbolically creating a sphere of protection and energy.

Cleansing

Purifying an object, space, or person energetically before magical or spiritual work.

Coven

A group of Wiccans who meet regularly for ritual and spiritual practice.

Craft

A common term for magical practice or Witchcraft.

Crone

The third aspect of the Triple Goddess, associated with wisdom, death, and transformation.

Deosil

Clockwise movement in ritual, symbolizing manifestation and positive energy.

Drawing Down the Moon

A ritual in which a priestess invokes the energy or presence of the Goddess into herself.

Earth

One of the four classical Elements; represents stability, grounding, growth, and physicality.

Elder

A respected teacher or practitioner with many years of experience in the Craft.

Elementals

Spiritual beings associated with the four Elements: gnomes (earth), sylphs (air), salamanders (fire), undines (water).

Elements

The four primary forces of nature—Earth, Air, Fire, and Water—plus Spirit as the fifth element.

Esbat

A ritual held on the Full Moon or other lunar phases, often for magical workings.

Evocation

Calling upon a spirit or deity to be present, often remaining external to the practitioner.

Familiar

A spiritual companion—animal, spirit, or thoughtform—that assists in magical practice.

Fire

One of the classical Elements; symbolizes transformation, passion, and willpower.

Grimoire

Another term for a magical journal or spellbook, sometimes used interchangeably with Book of Shadows.

Grounding

The practice of connecting to Earth energy to stabilize and balance oneself before or after ritual.

Handfasting

A Wiccan or Pagan marriage ceremony, sometimes temporary or renewable by design.

Herbalism

The magical and medicinal use of herbs in spells, charms, teas, and rituals.

High Priestess

A female ritual leader in a coven or circle, often one who embodies the Goddess in ritual.

High Priest

A male ritual leader in a coven or circle, often one who embodies the God in ritual.

Imbolc

A Sabbat celebrated on February 1 or 2, honoring the first signs of spring and the Goddess Brigid.

Incantation

A spoken or chanted phrase used to direct magical energy and focus intention.

Incense

Burned herbs or resins used in ritual for cleansing, invocation, or altering consciousness.

Initiation

A formal spiritual or magical rite of passage, welcoming someone into a tradition or level of practice.

Invocation

Calling a deity or spirit into ritual, often inviting them into the body or presence of a participant.

Lammas

A Sabbat celebrated on August 1, honoring the first harvest and the waning strength of the Sun God.

Litha

The Summer Solstice Sabbat, celebrating light, abundance, and the peak of solar power.

Magick

The intentional use of energy to cause change in accordance with will. Often spelled with a 'k' to distinguish it from stage magic.

Mabon

The Autumn Equinox Sabbat, marking balance between light and dark and giving thanks for the second harvest.

Maiden

The first aspect of the Triple Goddess, representing youth, new beginnings, and exploration.

Meditation

A practice of quiet reflection or focus used to calm the mind and attune to spirit or energy.

Ostara

The Spring Equinox Sabbat, celebrating renewal, fertility, and balance.

Pentacle

A five-pointed star within a circle, symbolizing the Elements and Spirit in harmony.

Ritual

A symbolic, structured act used to connect with the Divine, direct energy, or mark spiritual transitions.

Ritual Tools

Objects used during ritual to represent Elements, focus energy, and aid in magical workings (e.g., athame, wand, chalice).

Runes

Symbols from ancient alphabets used for divination, meditation, or magical inscriptions.

Sabbat

One of the eight seasonal festivals celebrated in the Wheel of the Year, marking natural cycles of light and harvest.

Salt

Used in ritual for purification, grounding, and protection. Often placed on altars or used in circle casting.

Samhain

A Sabbat celebrated on October 31, honoring the dead and marking the Witches' New Year.

Scourge

A symbolic ritual tool sometimes used in initiatory traditions to represent purification and humility.

Scrying

A form of divination using reflective surfaces like mirrors, water, or crystal balls to receive visions or insight.

Shadow Work

Spiritual and psychological work focused on acknowledging and integrating the hidden or repressed aspects of the self.

Shielding

A technique used to create energetic boundaries and protect oneself from negative or intrusive energy.

Sigil

A magical symbol charged with intention and used to manifest a specific desire or outcome.

Skyclad

Ritual nudity practiced in some traditions as a symbol of purity, vulnerability, or equality before the Divine.

Smudging

The practice of burning herbs (often sage) to cleanse space or individuals of stagnant or negative energy.

Solitary Practitioner

Someone who practices Wicca or Witchcraft alone, rather than as part of a group or coven.

Spirit

The fifth Element in Wicca, representing divine consciousness, unity, and the ineffable life force.

Spiritual Cleansing

Rituals performed to remove energetic blockages or attachments from a person or space.

Spell

A focused intention enacted through symbolic action and energy, aimed at creating change. Often viewed at the Wiccan version of prayer.

Staff

A ritual tool similar to a wand, often larger and associated with grounding or elemental work.

Talisman

An object charged to attract or hold a specific kind of energy, such as success, protection, or love.

Triple Goddess

A primary Wiccan deity form representing Maiden, Mother, and Crone aspects of the feminine divine.

Visualization

A magical technique involving mental imagery to direct energy, shape outcomes, or alter consciousness.

Wand

A ritual tool used to channel and direct energy, often associated with the Element of Air or Fire.

Ward

A magical barrier or protective boundary placed around people, objects, or spaces.

Watchtowers

Elemental guardians of the four cardinal directions called upon in formal ritual for protection and balance.

Waxing Moon

The period between the new moon and full moon, associated with growth, attraction, and new beginnings.

Waning Moon

The period between the full moon and new moon, associated with release, banishing, and reflection.

Wheel of the Year

The cyclical calendar of Wiccan Sabbats reflecting seasonal change and spiritual growth.

White Magic

Magic performed with benevolent intent, typically for healing, blessing, or protection.

Wicca

A modern Pagan religion centered on reverence for nature, the Divine in male and female form, and the practice of magic.

Wiccan Rede

The central ethical statement of Wicca: 'An it harm none, do what ye will.'

Widdershins

Counter-clockwise movement, often used in rituals of banishing or undoing.

Will

The focused intent of a practitioner, considered a central force in magical workings.

Yule

The Winter Solstice Sabbat, marking the rebirth of the Sun and the return of light.

Zodiac

The twelve astrological signs that influence personality and magical timing through planetary movements.

Glossary of Subsidiary terms

Altar Cloth

A cloth used to cover a ritual altar, often colored or decorated to suit the season or magical intention.

Arcana

In Tarot, the Major and Minor Arcana are the primary divisions of the deck's structure and symbolism.

Aspect

A version or face of a deity (e.g., Brigid as healer vs. Brigid as warrior).

Astral Travel

The experience of projecting one's consciousness into a non-physical plane or dreamscape.

Aurum Solis

A magical order with roots in Hermeticism and Western mystery traditions.

Binding Spell

A spell designed to restrict harmful actions, often cast for protection or ethical restraint.

Blood Moon

A full moon that appears red during a lunar eclipse; sometimes used for intense spiritual work.

Chant

Repetitive, rhythmic phrases used in ritual to raise energy or invoke a state of focus.

Cone of Power

The collective energy raised in group ritual and directed toward a shared magical goal.

Consecration

The act of ritually blessing or dedicating a tool, space, or person for sacred use.

Divination

The practice of seeking insight through symbolic systems like Tarot, runes, or pendulums.

Elemental Magic

Spellwork and rituals focused on invoking or balancing the powers of Earth, Air, Fire, and Water.

Goddess

The feminine aspect of the Divine in Wicca, often worshipped in her triple form: Maiden, Mother, Crone.

God

The masculine aspect of the Divine in Wicca, often associated with the Horned God or solar figures.

Mysticism

The pursuit of direct spiritual experience with the Divine or deeper truths beyond ordinary perception.

Pagan

A broad term for earth-centered spiritual paths that are often polytheistic or nature-based.

Ritual Bath

A symbolic cleansing using water and intention to purify the self before ritual or spellwork.

Solar Magic

Magic performed during daylight or focused on solar themes such as success, vitality, or clarity.

References

Part One – Chapter One:

Cordain, L., Miller, J.D., Eaton, S.D. *et al.* Plant-animal subsistence ratios and macronutrient energy estimations in worldwide hunter-gatherer diets. *The American Journal of Clinical Nutrition, Volume* 71, Issue 3, March 2000, Pages 682–692, https://doi.org/10.1093/ajcn/71.3.682.

d'Errico, F. & Nowell, A. A New Look at the Berekhat Ram Figurine:Implications for the Origins of Symbolism *Cambridge Archaeological Journal 10*:1 (2000), 123–67.

Weber, G.W., Lukeneder, A., Harzhauser, M. *et al.* The microstructure and the origin of the Venus from Willendorf. *Sci Rep* 12, 2926 (2022). https://doi.org/10.1038/s41598-022-06799-z.

Chapter Two:

Agency, A. Catalhoyuk home to figurines of old women, not goddesses. *Daily Sabah* January 16, 2017.

Ratnagar, S. (2016). A critical view of Marshall's Mother Goddess at Mohenjo-Daro. *Studies in People's History*, 3(2), 113–127. https://doi.org/10.1177/2348448916665714

Sanujit. Religious Developments in Ancient India. *World History Encyclopedia*. May 2011. https://www.worldhistory.org/article/230/religious-developments-in-ancient-india/

Tinning, J Is there a belief in the Mother Goddess at Catalhoyuk? *Catalhoyuk Research Project.* 01/13/2017. https://www.catalhoyuk.com/node/736

Chapter Three:

Behjati-Ardakani Z, Akhondi MM, Mahmoodzadeh H, Hosseini SH. An Evaluation of the Historical Importance of Fertility and Its Reflection in Ancient Mythology. J *Reprod Infertil.* 2016 Jan-Mar;17(1):2-9. PMID: 26962477; PMCID: PMC4769851.

Dukstra, M., (2001) El, the God of Israel – Israel the people of YHWH: On the Origins of Ancient Israelite Yahwism in *Only One God?: Monotheism in Ancient Israel and the Veneration of the Goddess Asherah* (Biblical Seminar) by Bob Becking, Meindert Dijkstra, Marjo C. A. Korpel, Karel J. H. Vriezen, Sheffield Academic Press 2001.

Fletcher-Stack, P., (2021, 9 May) Latter-day Saints are talking more about Heavenly Mother, and that's where the debates and divisions begin. *The Salt Lake Tribune.* https://www.sltrib.com/religion/2021/05/08/latter-day-saints-are/

Hausman, T. & Boggs, C., *Who is the Egyptian Goddess Isis? Origin, Facts, & Symbol.* Study.com 07/10/2022.

https://study.com/learn/lesson/egyptian-goddess-isis-origin-facts-symbol.html

Heiser, M Are Yahweh and El Distinct Deities in Deut 32:8-9 and Psalm 82?

LBTSFaculty Publications and Presentations. Published 2006

Hunt, L., (2001) *Celestial Goddesses.* St. Paul, Minnesota. Llewellyn Publications.

Kujawa, J., (n.d.) *Inanna-Ishtar, Isis, Mary Magdalene: Recovering the Lineage of the Lost Goddess and Other Stolen Stories.* Rebelle Society. https://rebellesociety.com/2018/05/16/joannakujawa-goddess-2/#:~:text=She%20was%20a%20goddess%20connecte

Mooney, J., (1966) *Myths of the Cherokee*. Washington, DC. Bureau of American Ethnology.

Noyce, D., (2016, 14 November). Meet the (heavenly) parents: Leaders of the church are mentioning this divine duo more often. *The Salt Lake Tribune*. https://archive.sltrib.com/article.php?id=4549096&itype=CMSID

Patai, R., The Goddess Asherah *Journal of Near Eastern Studies* 24(1-2), 37-52. University of Chicago Press. http://www.jstor.org/stable/543094

Rohrlich, R., (1980). State Formation in Sumer and the Subjugation of Women. *Feminist Studies*, 6(1), 76–102. https://doi.org/10.2307/3177651

Viegas, J., (March 18, 2011) God's Wife Edited Out of the Bible – Almost: God had a wife, Asherah, whom the Book of Kings suggests was worshiped alongside Yahweh in his temple in Israel, according to an Oxford scholar. NBC News. https://www.nbcnews.com/id/wbna42147912

Chapter Four:

Benz, E., (2009) *The Eastern Orthodox Church: Its Thought and Life.* Philadelphia, PA, Routledge Publishers.

Paulist Fathers, (1915) *Catholic World*, Volume 101. Digitized in the collection of Harvard University, November 1, 2007. P. 577.

Russell, J., (2000, December 23, 2000) Seeking a Promotion for the Virgin Mary. *The New York Times* https://www.nytimes.com/2000/12/23/arts/seeking-a-promotion-for-the-virgin-mary.html[1]

Santa Veneranda, 2006, Santi e beati. https://www.santiebeati.it/dettaglio/90950

Van Oort, J., (2016) The Holy Spirit as feminine: Early Christian testimonies and their interpretation *HTS Theological Studies* Vol. 72 (1) http://dx.doi.org/10.4102/hts.v72i1.3225

---

1. https://www.nytimes.com/2000/12/23/arts/seeking-a-promotion-for-the-virgin-mary.h

Chapter Five:

Oehrl, S and Ljung C (nd) *Traces of pagan heritage in Swedish churches.* Marcus and Amalia Wallenberg Foundation. Retrieved August 13, 2024 from: https://maw.wallenberg.org/en/traces-pagan-heritage-swedish-churches

Pagliarulo, A. (October, 30, 2022) *Why Paganism and witchcraft are making a comeback.* NBC News. Retrieved August 13, 2024 from: cnews.com/think/opinion/paganism-witchcraft-are-making-comeback-rcna54444[1]

Starhawk (1981) *The Spiral Dance: A Rebirth of the Ancient Religion of the Great Goddess.* New York, NY. Harper and Row Publishers.

---

1. http://cnews.com/think/opinion/paganism-witchcraft-are-making-comeback-rcna54444

Chapter Six:

Jordan, M (1999) *New World Encyclopedia & Witches: An Encyclopedia of Paganism and Magic.* London, UK. Kyle Cathie Ltd

Marchetti, K (2022) A Political Profile of US Pagans. *Politics and Religion, Volume 15* (1) pp. 142-168. DOI: https://doi.org/10.1017/S17550483210000055

Part Two –
Chapter Eight:

Winnick, S. (April 18, 2016) *Ostara and the Hare: Not Ancient, but Not As Modern As Some Skeptics Think.* Library of Congress Blogs. Retrieved October 20, 2024 from: https://blogs.loc.gov/folklife/2016/04/ostara-and-the-hare/#:~:text=As%20I%20detailed%20in%20the,1%5D [1]

Afterword –

When I started this project two years ago, my idea was to create a comprehensive book that briefly covered the history and prehistory of goddess worship, discussed how that gave rise to modern Wicca and then delved into the nature of what Wicca was, and how Wiccans worshiped. I thought it would be fairly simple and straight forward to complete. I was wrong. I have spent over a thousand hours researching, writing, checking facts multiple times and pulling together this book, of which I am moderately proud.

As is discussed in the book, Wicca is the fastest growing religion, by percentage, in the world. If it extends to what appear to be its outer margins, it will rival the largest of the Christian churches in the West and will eventually, over time, force acceptance in other parts of the world, with the possible exception of theocracies and theonomies.[42]

Given these facts, it is important that there be a general understanding of what Wicca is, how Wiccans worship, and what Wiccans believe in. It is not enough to laugh at those who are not part of the faith and make false claims, for that only frightens them more - and make no mistake - they are frightened. I know that it seems farcical, but they are, and that is something that needs to be addressed, corrected, and healed.

Wicca is a religion. For many it is an earth based religion, but some who follow it are less earth based than others. There are branches, denominations, and different ritual practices as we have seen - exactly as there are in other major faith traditions.

I hope you have enjoyed this book, and that it helps you better understand the path that you have chosen, or that someone you know has chosen. There is really nothing to be afraid of in Wicca. It simply acknowledges the divine feminine again, as well as the divine masculine; something that has been acknowledged in thousands of years. It does not worship, or even believe, in demons or devils. It is, without question, a peaceful, caring, and gentle faith.

This book is web enabled, and going to http://www.whywicca.com and then to the page tilted "web-enabled" will give you access to a few special gifts for its purchasers. The password is *moonfire25*.

Thank you for your time, your purchase, and your fellowship.

Kind thoughts,

Rowan Antinous

Resources –

The following books, websites, and tools are recommended for Wiccans at all stages of the path. Some offer foundational teachings, others delve into specific traditions or practices. Always read with discernment, and follow your intuition to what resonates most deeply with your journey.

Foundational Books on Wicca

- *Wicca: A Guide for the Solitary Practitioner* by Scott Cunningham
- *The Spiral Dance* by Starhawk
- *The Witch's Book of Shadows* by Phyllis Curott
- *Witchcraft Today* by Gerald Gardner
- *Wicca for Beginners* by Thea Sabin
- *The Triumph of the Moon* by Ronald Hutton (historical perspective)

Books on Magic, Ritual, and Spellwork

- *Earth Power* and *Earth, Air, Fire & Water* by Scott Cunningham
- *The Elements of Ritual* by Deborah Lipp
- *A Witch's Guide to Ritual* by Kala Trobe
- *The Inner Temple of Witchcraft* by Christopher Penczak
- *Spellcraft for Beginners* by Mickie Mueller

Herbalism, Crystals, and Divination

- *Cunningham's Encyclopedia of Magical Herbs* by Scott Cunningham
- *The Crystal Bible* by Judy Hall

- *Encyclopedia of 5,000 Spells* by Judika Illes
- *The Tarot Bible* by Sarah Bartlett
- *The Complete Book of Tarot Reversals* by Mary K. Greer

Advanced and Philosophical Works

- *Drawing Down the Moon* by Margot Adler
- *The Temple of Shamanic Witchcraft* by Christopher Penczak
- *Evolutionary Witchcraft* by T. Thorn Coyle
- *When God Was a Woman* by Merlin Stone
- *The Witch's Eight Paths of Power* by Lady Sable Aradia

Online Communities and Resources

- [The Witches' Voice Archive (witchvox.com)](https://witchvox.com) – Historical community networking resource

- [Sacred-texts.com](https://sacred-texts.com) – Public domain esoteric texts

- [Pagan Pride Project](https://paganpride.org) – Community outreach and events

- [Patheos Pagan Channel](https://www.patheos.com/Pagan) – Blogs and essays from a wide range of traditions

Tools and Reference

- Tarot or Oracle Decks: Choose imagery that speaks to you
- Moon Phase Apps: Time Passages, Deluxe Moon, or MoonX
- Journals and Blank Books: For your Book of Shadows or personal reflections

- **Digital Tools:** Note-taking apps, ritual timers, lunar calendars, and astrology software

Websites and Contact Information –

http://www.whywicca.com – the book site, which included the web-enabled gifts for purchasers. On the front page is a Premium Content button. The passcode is moonfire25.

Email to reach the author: author@whywicca.com.

http://www.whywicca.store – a store maintained for all of your needs as a Wiccan or neoPagan practitioner.

Email to reach someone in the store: info@whywicca.store

http://www.exultans.com – the website for the publisher.

Email to reach the publisher: info@exultans.com

https://www.newaeonchurch.org/ – the website for the Omnistic Church that endorses this book. (The Church has an Order of Wicca, and other specific orders, including one for LGBTQA persons.

Email to reach the church: admin@newaeonchurch.org

Ash can be

M

accurately dated, unlike rock.

[1] One suppor

ing evidence for the divine character of the many goddess figurines from the Stone Age is, according to the Brooklyn Museum, that Paleolithic and Neolithic people did not have enough fatty foods in their diets to attain such weight, unless pregnant, and often not then.

[2] Leopards a

e frequently represented in the city, with one goddess actually riding a leopard.

[3] Scholarly

onsensus is that the Torah, from which all Abrahamic religions ultimately flow was not collated and written down until at least 700 BCE and possibly as late as 300 BCE.

[4] For those

ho may not realize, Lord Shiva, in Hinduism, is symbolized as an erect phallus. The lingam in Hindu temples are representative of Shiva's penis.

[5] Henotheism

is the belief that there are many gods, but your people only worship one of them. So, Israel was henotheistic until at least the end of the Babylonian captivity and most experts think later than that. They worshiped YHWH (Yahweh) but they recognized that the other gods and goddesses of the Levant existed. One does not compare a real thing to a non-existent thing - but yet, the scriptures are clear when they say things like: Psalm 97:9 says *"For thou Lord art high above the Earth. Thou art exalted **far above all gods**."*

(KJV, emphasis added). Exodus 15:11 says *"Who is like unto thee O Lord* ***among the gods?*** *Who is like thee glorious in holiness, fearful in praises, doing wonders!?"* (KJV, emphasis added). 1 Kings 8:23 says *"And he said 'Lord God of Israel,* ***there is no god like thee in heaven above or on earth beneath*** *who keepest thy covenant with thy servants that walk before thee with all thy heart."* (KJV, emphasis added) Psalm 86:8 *"****There is no one like You among the gods****, O Lord, Nor are there any works like Yours."* (ESV, emphasis added). All of these verses clearly indicate (along with a host of other passages) that the early Jews were not monotheistic. They were henotheistic. Many groups were. They did not believe that their god was the only god, anymore than the Moabites believed the Chemosh was the only god. They worshiped their god and followed them and served them as they understood and they expected to be rewarded.

[6] Asherah is

mentioned in the Bible and is generally viewed as being a Canaanite Goddess, whose titles included "she who walks on the sea" and "The Goddess." According to Ugaritic texts, Asherah's consort was El, and by him she mothered 70 gods. The Hebrew Bible, collated after the Hebrew faith became determined to make the final jump to monotheism (in part to strengthen the position of monarchs) downplayed her position to that of a "sacred pole" of a pagan (meaning not Jewish) religion. However, the Book of Kings seems to suggest that she was worshiped along with Yahweh in his temple, and strong evidence has been found backing that, in the form of inscriptions in Hebrew from the temple period, asking for the blessings of both Yahweh and Asherah - as a divine couple.

[7] The date o

the earliest prayer to Mary of which we still have a copy - *the Sub tuum praesidium* - is argued by many manuscript experts to be ~250 CE. Some have tried to argue that it dates to the 800s, however, as it has been found in the Georgian Iadgari, a chantbook used in the 400s, it certainly dates to at least that early.

[8] Brigid: "xalted One."

[9] Tuatha De anann: Usually translated as "tribe of the gods" - it appears extremely likely that they are also the fey (fairies). It is suggested that the fey known as the Sidhe {shee} were originally the Tuatha de Danann, driven underground by violent tribes of humans [Sidhe means "People of the Underground.]

[10] Kildare: "hurch of the Oak." The oaks were older than the church built there, and word of mouth legend relates that the Druids worshiped in the grove of oaks where the church ultimately stood.

[11] February 1 is Brigid's day which continues on February 2 with the pagan celebration of Imbolc, which became the Christian celebration of Candlemas.

[12] Many acadeics and skeptics seek to find a way to deny Gardner's claim of initiation in an existing group. They examine ritual forms and claim they came from the Masons, or the Rosicrucians, or whatever else. They deny that such a group as Gardner claimed to initiate him ever could have existed. Basically, they run their mouths a lot. Reality is that all pre-Christian religions in Europe share a lot of similarities, the secret orders that arose among the Christians share those similarities as well. I personally see no reason not to take him at his word.

[13] While it i true, as the media has reported, that there are White Supremacist Heathen, there are far more non-racist, inclusive and receiving Heathen.

[14] The Law of

Three is believed by Wiccans to be a cosmic law. What you do to help others, returns to you three times over, but what you do to harm others, also returns three times over.

[15] If you use

ritual tools (such as athames, pentacles, candles, chalices, etc.), it's important to cleanse them before using them in rituals to ensure they carry positive energy. (*footnote continued next page.*)

> M **Smudging:** Pass each tool through the smoke of sage, palo santo, or other cleansing herbs.
>
> M **Salt and Water:** You can cleanse tools by placing them in a bowl of salt or using a cloth dampened with water to wipe them down.
>
> M **Sound:** You can use sound, such as a bell or chimes, to clear the energy of an object. Simply ring the bell over the object or tool.

[16] **Directiona**

ity: In Wicca, some people orient their altar to face a particular direction, depending on the type of ritual or the deities they are working with. For example, the **God** might be placed on the **right** (symbolizing the masculine), while the **Goddess** is placed on the **left** (representing the feminine). However, this is not a strict rule and can be customized based on personal preference. (continued)

Personalization: A temporary altar can be as simple or elaborate as you choose. You can incorporate personal items that hold significance to you or that align with the particular energy you wish to invoke.

After Ritual: Once your ritual is complete, you can thank the deities, close the circle, and either leave the altar intact for later work or take everything down to store until needed again.

[17] A more ritualistic and formalized invocation might be something like "Guardians of the Watchtowers of the East, Lords of Air, we welcome you to our rite tonight and ask your protection and guidance." This formula has been influenced over the centuries by ceremonial magic, but the intent is the same. The other directions would follow a similar pattern.

[18] a ritual method for raising energy that involves a group of people standing in a circle and focusing on a single point. The cone of power is visualized as a cone of energy that extends from the circle to a point above the group and the energy in the cone is then directed by will to its stated purpose.

[19] For example, in a Fey Ritual (see chapter on sample rituals) I have seen a solitary, dressed in ritual robes and cloak with a longsword for cutting the circle, literally sprawl face down in the direction of the Seelie Court (generally seen to be either East) and plead, cajole, beg the Queen of the Fey to aid his cause. I cannot say that it was her, but something acted and a very dangerous situation was resolved for his friend.

[20] The ritual as I have heard it generally has some variation on the following: (holding up the bread or cake) "By the bounty of the Lady, may you never hunger" and then (holding up the drink) "By the bounty of the Lord may you never thirst." In some groups a third voice then adds "By the presence of the ancestors, may you never be alone." It is profoundly moving. The first time I saw the ceremony was close to 20 years ago now, and I was immediately reminded of Eucharist and felt that it was a more earthly version of the same, which probably predated its use in Christianity and perhaps even precursor religions.

[21] None of th

groups that I am personally familiar with use alcohol. All of the groups have minor children in attendance, and most of them also have people who do not imbibe alcohol. They use fruit juice instead.

[22] In my pers

nal experience they are scattered, as a gift to nature and in the case of one group - to the fey.

[23] Ditto

[24] Either on

he altar if it is permanent, or in a safe location if it a temporary altar that you are removing all traces of until its next use.

[25] The Flamek

epers are an order within the Church of the New Aeon's Wiccan branch.

[26] Done by th

children in two of the groups that I have attended.

[27] This formu

ae is the opposite of the standard formulae that research tells me is more common in Wiccan circles, in that the food item is associated with the God and the drink item associated with the Goddess. The reason for this is the God's association with the sun - which allows harvesting of grain, while the Goddess, in her form as matron (mother) - the second form of the Goddess (Maid, Matron, Chrome) is the source of liquid nourishment for Her offspring.

[28] Hermetic r

tuals are esoteric practices rooted in the ancient Hermetic tradition, often combining elements of alchemy, astrology, theurgy, and other occult disciplines, with the goal of achieving spiritual transformation by aligning the practitioner with the divine order and unlocking hidden knowledge about the universe and oneself through symbolic rituals and practices, often involving specific tools and correspondences to different celestial and spiritual energies; they are considered a blend of philosophy and ritualistic practices aimed at personal spiritual development and understanding the interconnectedness of all things. The ritual sequence for the equinoxes is similar, and so I am including the variant here for those interested.

[29] Chaos prac

ice is almost always solitary and is only tangentially attached to Wicca. Since it is viewed as Wiccan by many people, we are including a set of their ritual outlines, though that may be an overstatement. Chaos practice is much more a magical route than a method of worshipping deity, in my personal view. But, since it is viewed as being a branch of Wicca, it is appropriate to cover it.

[30] **A Wiccan C**

ming of Age Ritual is a sacred and transformative ceremony that marks an individual's transition from childhood or adolescence into adulthood, both spiritually and personally. It is a celebration of growth, self-awareness, and readiness to take on new responsibilities within the Wiccan or Pagan community. This ritual often includes reaffirming one's connection with the Goddess and God, as well as the elements and nature. The ritual can be customized based on personal or family traditions.

[31] Such tasks

should be chosen very carefully and with an eye to being both doable, and clearly symbolic, not extraneous.

[32] A **Wiccan H**

ndfasting is a sacred ceremony of commitment, often described as a union of two individuals or two souls. It is a Wiccan wedding. In Wicca, the ceremony is rooted in the elements, nature, and divine balance, emphasizing the sacredness of love and partnership. I'll offer a **Wiccan Handfasting Ritual**, with possible alterations for "non traditional" (same-sex) marriages. In any event, the ritual can be personalized based on the couple's preferences and beliefs.

[33] The Rite

elebrates the Elder's connection to the divine, their wisdom, and the continuity of the spiritual teachings they carry. It reinforces the idea that elders are vital links between the past, present, and future, and their legacy continues to guide the spiritual and communal journey. **Elder** may be chosen as a gender-neutral term; **Crone** may be chosen by women; **Sage** may be chosen by men. Usually held for women after the completion of menopause and for men at 60.

[34] The Wiccan

approach to death is rooted in the belief that life is cyclical, and death is merely a transition. These rites are focused on guiding the soul to the next realm with love, honoring the deceased's journey, and celebrating their life. The rituals help the community move through their grief while affirming the belief in eternal connection and the continuous cycle of life, death, and rebirth. (please see chapter on beliefs.)

[35] Generally,

if it is at all possible the celebrant should be a priest. Likewise for the Mother, the celebrant should be a priestess.

[36] The Wiccan

Hand-Parting Ritual is about honoring the past while creating space for the future. It is an opportunity to acknowledge the shared experiences of a relationship, express gratitude, and move forward with peace and clarity.

The ritual should be approached with an open heart, free from blame or bitterness, and with an intention to heal and release. It is not about severing ties completely, but about creating a healthy boundary that allows each individual to grow in their own direction.

[37] *Personal N*

te from the author – this ritual is included because of the enormous respect and love I had/have for Ruthann, may she rest in Light and return to the Wheel renewed. She told me this needed to be here a few months before her passing. I hold two Christian, one Universalist/Interfaith and one Metaphysical ordination, as well as my ordination in New Aeon. I have performed dozens of marriages through my time, and when any have ended, I have sorrowed for them, and felt that somehow I failed in preparing them. This ritual, I hope it helps people, but writing it and including it was the only difficult thing about researching and writing this book. I respectfully thank you for allowing me the time to say this.

[38] A copy for

atted for a handout appropriate to either teaching, or performing a blessing on ritual tools is included in Appendix Three - Miscellaneous Documents.

[39] While the

raditional phraseology is Book of Shadows, some modern practitioners are not comfortable with that due to potential reverberations of the name, and some choose instead to keep a Book of Lights.

[40] The Church

of the New Aeon, International, welcomes circles of Wiccans to become part of our Omnistic structure, to be chartered by the Church and to function under its umbrella. Please do not hesitate to contact our Paramount Priest directly, through the contacts section at the end of the book.

[41] a system o

government or social organization where civil law is based on and guided by divine law as understood by those governing. This is as opposed to a theocracy, where there is no civil law, but only religious law.

Antinous

Ant

www.ingramcontent.com/pod-product-compliance
Lightning Source LLC
Chambersburg PA
CBHW020738160426
43192CB00006B/232